C

S

& (

VGM Careers for You Series

CAREERS FOR

CYBER-SURFERS

& Other Online Types

MARJORIE EBERTS
RACHEL KELSEY

SECOND EDITION

VGM Career Books

Chicago   New York   San Francisco   Lisbon   London   Madrid   Mexico City
Milan   New Delhi   San Juan   Seoul   Singapore   Sydney   Toronto

1 2 3 4 5 6 7 8 9 0   LBM/LBM   2 1 0 9 8 7 6 5 4 3

ISBN 0-07-141146-1

McGraw-Hill books are available at special quantity discounts to use as premiums and sales promotions, or for use in corporate training programs. For more information, please write to the Director of Special Sales, Professional Publishing, McGraw-Hill, Two Penn Plaza, New York, NY 10121-2298. Or contact your local bookstore.

This book is printed on acid-free paper.

To Mary and Jane, who introduced us to the Internet world. Thank you for keeping in touch with your daily E-mail messages.

Contents

Acknowledgments

The authors wish to thank Kevin Crider for his online research in updating this book. He is a true cybersurfer who knows his way around the Internet.

CHAPTER ONE

An Introduction to the Internet and Online Careers

The world is going online, and it's going online at warp speed. Ten percent of the people in the world have access to the Internet. In the next few years, a billion people will be Net users, and 200 million of those cybersurfers will be in the United States and Canada. Within these two countries, Europe, and parts of Asia, going online has changed from being an unusual research tool to a routine, if not essential, part of life.

In the United States, the telephone is now taking a backseat to the Internet as the way teenagers are communicating with their friends. Online shopping is growing faster than mall shopping. Millions of workers have stopped going to work at the office and are now telecommuting from their homes. And just about every business of any size now has an online presence. Students are using the vast resources of the Internet to do their homework. Their parents are searching for medical advice, getting stock quotes, ordering food, and looking for jobs. There's a hermit in Egypt who is E-mailing the progress of an archaeological dig to American school children. There's a surfer in Australia going aboard the Net for surf reports. Queen Elizabeth II of England has her own website. The world is truly at the fingertips of all cybersurfers. Just about every activity has expanded or moved operations to the Internet. All of this is great news for cybersurfers who want Internet-related careers, as the list of possible choices is constantly growing.

What Is the Internet?

The Internet, also known as the Net, is the largest computer network in the world. It isn't a single network, but a network of networks with high-speed connections. There are tens of thousands of these networks ranging in size from the big networks of corporate giants to small home networks with just a couple of PCs to everything in between. The number of these networks is constantly growing. Every time you go aboard the Net, your own computer becomes an extension of that network. The Internet is similar to a telephone system in that it makes instant communication possible from place to place around the world.

Main Features of the Internet

One of the Internet's primary features is the World Wide Web (WWW), or Web, as it is frequently called. Although Tim Berners-Lee invented the Web in 1989, it was not until 1993, with the development of the Mosaic Web Browser, that people could truly navigate it. Today, when people talk about "surfing the Net," they are usually talking about using the World Wide Web. What makes the Web the most appealing and fastest-growing part of the Internet are the home pages with their graphics and sound. You can jump from any place on the Web to any other place by clicking on a hypertext link (onscreen button, image, or line of text). The language that makes all of this possible is hypertext markup language (HTML). HTML also tells your Web browser how to display the contents of a page.

The most widely used feature of the Internet is electronic mail (E-mail). Any cybersurfer with access to the Internet can exchange messages with anyone else on an Internet-connected system. The popularity of E-mail is astounding. It is rapidly replacing the interoffice memo at businesses and even replacing the telephone and mail as the way families and friends communicate with each other. In the United States, it will soon be the norm to have an E-mail address just as it is to have a telephone number today.

A Brief History of the Internet

Historically, the Internet is very young. It grew out of the Department of Defense's desire in the 1960s to keep military sites in communication in the event of an enemy attack. What evolved was the Advanced Research Projects Administration Network (ARPANET), a network in which electronic traffic could be rerouted in case one of the network links was damaged or destroyed. It connected military sites, defense contractors, and colleges and universities. Soon other networks were developed, and operators began asking permission to connect their networks to ARPANET.

The next major event in Internet history was the establishment of a much faster network, NSFNET, by the National Science Foundation in 1986 to connect supercomputer centers for research use. Then the foundation set up regional networks to link the users in each region, with the NSFNET connecting all the regional networks. Because NSFNET did not exclude people and institutions as ARPANET did, it was easy to become part of this network simply by getting a connection to someone who was connected. Soon the network wasn't just being used for research but also for E-mail, newsgroups, and file transfer; large commercial networks began building their own networks, which they linked to NSFNET. The new network grew so rapidly and assumed so many functions of ARPANET that the old network shut down in 1990.

By 1994, commercial firms had taken over the operation of the major network arteries, now collectively referred to as the Internet, and NSFNET was shut down a year later. In 1995, Amazon.com started selling books on the Internet, and eBay was launched as an online marketplace. Thousands of entrepreneurs were soon online, and E-commerce had become a reality. Suddenly, there was an explosion of dot-com activity, and new businesses associated with the Internet were starting up at breakneck speed to sell all kinds of products and services. Employees at these firms were given stock options as incentives, and when companies went public, even secretaries were becoming millionaires. Unfortunately, many of these companies were spending far more than they were making, and the financing of Internet companies began to dry up in 2000. This was quickly followed by the dot-com bust. Many start-ups failed, others went into holding patterns with fewer employees, and some merged with stronger companies. By the start of 2003, a strong group of Internet company survivors began to emerge, and the Internet was starting to become a more mature industry.

Internet Jobs—So Many Choices for Cybersurfers

The Internet industry is now a career destination. And just like other industries, the number of jobs depends on the state of the economy. When the economy is booming, hiring accelerates, and during downturns there are layoffs and pink slips. But despite the downturn of the economy early in the twenty-first century, the future is actually quite bright for those who wish to find a job associated with the Net.

Although the popular perception may be that most Net jobs are with dot-com companies, this simply isn't true. Dot-com companies have only a small share of all Internet-related jobs. There are jobs with online service providers, hardware and software companies, online and print newspapers and magazines, information services, colleges, libraries, and especially with all the "old line" companies that want to have a Net presence. Of course, many jobs that cybersurfers want are in information technology. Nevertheless, the number one area for Internet-related jobs is sales and marketing. The five occupations with the top growth rates, according to the U.S. Bureau of Labor Statistics, are computer engineering, technical support, systems analysis, database administration, and desktop publishing—all jobs that are found in Internet and Internet-related businesses.

The list of Internet-related jobs is very long. In the next eight chapters, you will learn what some of these jobs are. Caution: the Internet is still changing rapidly. You need to surf the Net to keep abreast of all the new career opportunities that are constantly emerging. Make this book an interactive experience by visiting the sites given in the text. This will enhance what you learn about careers for cybersurfers. Here is a brief overview of some of the careers you will read about in this book.

Getting Connected to the Internet

Providing access to the Internet is an area in which there is strong demand for qualified cybersurfers who truly understand this new medium. The demand is high for both "techies" and administrative types. While you probably are well acquainted with giant online service providers such as America Online, Microsoft, and Prodigy, jobs are also available at much smaller regional and local providers, as well as with network access companies, backbone operators, and large businesses.

Providing the Proper Hardware

Those who are part of creating Internet hardware typically work at one of the major equipment vendors, such as Cisco Systems or Nortel Networks, or at a line provider, such as AT&T or SBC. Hardware engineers are actively involved in the design and development of hardware. Assemblers, inspectors, technicians, production staff, product managers, quality-control experts, sales and marketing people, education specialists, technical writers, and maintenance people also play key roles in providing the hardware needed for the Internet. This is an exciting area because hardware is continuously being created and modified as developments in technology offer new choices.

Software: Making the Hardware Work

It is the software that makes the Internet and computer equipment work. And the people who write the software programs to make it all function are computer software engineers, systems analysts, computer scientists, database administrators, and computer programmers. While many of these jobs require a four-year degree, some only require completion of community college or technical institute programs. Because software careers often involve working as part of a team, you need solid oral and written communication skills to work in this area. An excellent way to enter this field is through a job as an intern.

Making the Net Accessible for Companies

It has become almost a requirement for companies to have an Internet presence. It takes a number of people to put both large and small companies online and to keep their websites up and running. Developing and maintaining websites creates many jobs in marketing, advertising, sales, and consulting, as well as in technical areas providing the necessary hardware, software, and programming. You could work within a company itself or for another company that provides Internet services for other organizations. There are also jobs for consultants and independent contractors.

Working as a Webmaster

Webmasters are in charge of the day-to-day operations of websites as well as their development. Frequently, they work with a team consisting of marketing, technical, content, and public relations specialists. Webmaster responsibilities vary depending on where they work, the size of the company or organization, or whether they own their own businesses. In any case, webmasters always have the ultimate responsibility of making sure that websites project the presence that companies wish to have on the Net.

Finance, Entertainment, and Other Net Service Careers

Help a person use the Internet to pay a bill, rent a car, reserve a movie ticket, find a job, take a college course, play a game, check a bank balance, learn more about a sports hero, or plan a trip—these are just a few of the unique services available on the Internet, and more are constantly coming aboard. Be a technical wizard and help a service be delivered to cybersurfers. Or you can do such things as create, promote, market, or help customers use the service. You'll find jobs at such diverse places as banks, brokerage houses, online employment agencies, newspapers and magazines, and universities.

E-Commerce Careers
Cybersurfers are beginning to get in the habit of shopping online. They have discovered that just about every product available in bricks-and-mortar stores is now being sold online, as well as some products that aren't even in stores. The expectation is that online shopping will skyrocket in the years ahead, which will create great opportunities for entrepreneurs who want to start their own businesses and for those who want to work for Internet businesses as well as traditional stores with online shopping options.

Education, Media, Research, and Other Online Careers
Everyday activities are rapidly moving to the Internet. Students are getting college degrees online without ever stepping into a classroom. People are reading magazines and newspapers on computer screens, doing research on their computers instead of going to the local library—even paying their taxes online. Each activity that goes online creates jobs for cybersurfers interested in the technical side of setting up and keeping the activity online.

The Internet and Future Opportunities
No one can predict the future with 100 percent accuracy. People were not able to guess at all the new jobs that appeared after the invention of the automobile, telephone, or television. The scenario is the same for Internet jobs.

Finding an Internet Job

Cybersurfers seeking a job associated with the Internet—or any other job—should use the Internet as part of their search. The career resources of the Net are stupendous. You will find huge databases of job listings and be able to search for a job any time, twenty-four hours a day, seven days a week. It's now just as easy to find out what jobs are available in Buffalo, New York, as in Berlin. You can post your resume in databases where prospective employers will see it, or you can send it by E-mail. You can network with other cybersurfers to find out about companies and possible job openings. You can even "chat" with career counselors and practice your interview skills online. Plus, the Internet offers the opportunity to research what a company is like and what types of jobs it offers. An additional advantage in using the Internet for a job search is that it lets you explore a wide variety of careers. And if prospective employers see your resume online, they will know that you are Net savvy.

Don't put all your apples in one basket, however. You cannot use only the Internet to find a job—even if it is one associated with the Net. A good job search also involves:

- contacting companies about possible job vacancies
- networking
- getting job leads from newspapers, magazines, college placement services, and associations

You also may find a job by attending career fairs, conventions, and trade shows. Professional and trade journals may have listings for jobs that appeals to you. And don't forget about contacting an employment agency.

One of the very best resources for job seekers wanting to use the Internet to their advantage is *The Riley Guide*, available online at www.rileyguide.com. It is an award-winning directory of employment and career information sources and services on the Internet that provides instruction on how to use the Internet in your career search. Two good print resources include *The Guide to Internet Job Searching* by Margaret Riley Dikel and Frances Roehm and *Job Searching Online for Dummies* by Pam Dixon.

Applying for Jobs Advertised on the Internet

Many employers are now asking job applicants to apply by E-mail. If you are going to apply for a job online, you need an online resume in plain text. It is not the print version of your resume, but one that is specially done so it looks good after it has been E-mailed or posted to a job website. To learn how to write an online resume, visit *The Riley Guide* website mentioned previously or read one of the following books: *Resumes for Dummies* by Joyce Lain Kennedy or *Internet Resumes* by Peter D. Weddle. After you have completed your online resume, always E-mail it to yourself or a friend to check how it looks.

How Much Can You Expect to Earn?

The easiest way to find salary information on jobs associated with the Internet is to use the Net. Go to www.rileyguide.com to find lists of sites with salary information. Two sites that are very helpful are www.jobstar.org and www.salary.com. You can also receive salary information at some trade and professional association websites. When you find the information you want, be sure to evaluate it in terms of how current it is, its geographic coverage, and your own situation.

Qualifications for Internet Jobs

Organizations will not hire you just because you enjoy surfing the Net; however, your ability to move skillfully around the Internet is a tremendous plus for so many jobs. Internet companies, as well as businesses that are on the Net, respect college degrees. A degree in computer science or computer engineering is a solid ticket to a job in any market. If you are not working in a position developing Net hardware or software, a technical major is not necessary. However, computer literacy is a requirement for almost every job, and this includes knowing how to use E-mail and to navigate the Internet. Companies are also very interested in hiring people with experience. Both paid and unpaid internships are excellent paths to getting your foot in the door at many companies.

CHAPTER TWO

Getting Connected to the Internet

Providing access to the Internet has become a highly competitive industry. Companies and individuals are clamoring for connections that are both fast and secure. There is intense competition among access providers to sign up new customers by offering specialized services and a range of access speeds. Overall, there is a tremendous need for qualified people who understand the new medium. From technicians to software engineers, from service representatives to marketing professionals, there is strong demand for people at the companies that provide access to the Internet.

An Overview of Access Providers

When you first think of a job associated with offering Internet access, you may immediately think of working at an online service provider, such as America Online or Microsoft Network. These companies, however, are decidedly not the only ones involved in providing Net access. To know where all the jobs are in this area, you need to understand how the Internet is built.

Traffic speeds across the Internet on backbones, or very high-capacity lines. Network access points (NAPs) offer interconnections to national and regional backbone operators. The backbone operators in turn offer connections to the online service providers, Internet service providers, and large businesses. Consumers and smaller businesses generally connect to a service

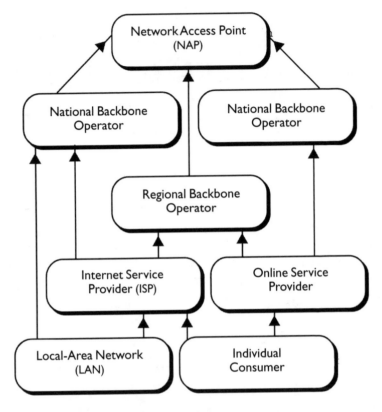

FIGURE 2.1. Internet Traffic Pattern

provider. Figure 2.1 shows how traffic flows on the Internet. You can find jobs with NAPs, backbone operators, online service providers, Internet service providers, and large businesses.

Network Access Points

The NAPs provide the basis for interconnectivity between the backbone operators. They are the physical points where the backbones connect and exchange information. There are four official NAPs as well as seven other major interconnection points that perform the same function. The following websites offer information on the NAPs, and most include descriptions of available jobs.

Big East NAP: ICS Network Systems
www.bigeast.net

Chicago and San Francisco NAP: SBC Communications
www.sbc.com

New York NAP: Sprint
www.sprint.com

Washington, D.C., NAP: MCI
www.mci.com

Bell South
www.bellsouth.com

United States Internet Service Provider Association
www.cix.org

National and Regional Backbone Operators

Companies that function as backbone operators have high-speed TCP/IP (transfer control protocol/Internet protocol) routers connected by data transmission lines leased from long-distance exchange carriers. They usually connect several major cities with high-speed leased lines and extend those connections to surrounding areas with slower lines. This creates a network that is often made up of several hundred cities and towns.

The backbones offer direct connections to businesses and Internet service providers through machines called gateways, or IP routers, which are continuously online. These are expensive connections requiring a heavy initial outlay for equipment and software as well as ongoing costs for leasing dedicated telephone lines and providing continuing support. In addition to offering dedicated connections, the backbones may also contain divisions that act as service providers.

Major Backbone Operators

Visit the websites of some of the major backbone operators to learn more about the services they provide. Many also offer information about employment opportunities.

Ardent	www.ardentcomm.com
AT&T	www.ipservices.att.com/backbone
Infonet	www.infonet.com
ICG Communications	www.icgcom.com
Qwest	www.qwest.com
Sprint	www.sprint.com
PSINet	www.psinet.com
MCI (UUNet)	www.mci.com
Time Warner Telecom	www.twtelecom.com

National Internet Service Providers

National Internet service providers (ISPs) are the large commercial services such as America Online, Microsoft Network, CompuServe, and Prodigy. You are probably familiar with these names. These services are traditionally the first access points for the beginning online explorer. They offer a great deal of general-interest information and family-oriented content, provide E-mail and World Wide Web access, and offer a browser to navigate the Net. Ease of installation is a plus for beginners.

The major online providers are to some degree distinguished by the types of services they offer. America Online offers access to national magazines and search databases. Microsoft features speed of service with fewer busy signals. CompuServe, which was bought by AOL in 1998, specializes in first-time adult users, and Prodigy, which is owned by SBC, features graphics-based multi-play games and general news. On the negative side, the services offer only an indirect connection; their computers are interposed between the customer and the Internet, exerting a controlling influence on the information exchange.

The growth of ISPs has mirrored the growth of the Internet. Competition to acquire customers is intense. Further information about the major online service providers and employment opportunities at these companies is available at the following websites:

America Online	www.aol.com
Microsoft	www.msn.com
CompuServe	www.compuserve.com
Prodigy	http://myhome.prodigy.net

A National Internet Service Provider

America Online (AOL) was founded in 1985 and is now a division of the Time Warner media empire. AOL serves more than thirty-five million customers throughout the United States and overseas, reaching more than 60 percent of the U.S. Internet audience. The average customer is online about seventy minutes a day, and total usage is more than one billion hours per month. AOL currently serves about one-third of U.S. dial-up accounts but only about 3 percent of the broadband subscriptions. As revenues from broadband subscriptions are expected to soon be greater than those from dial-up accounts, AOL's relative position in the online market is under pressure. The company is heavily marketing broadband connections that offer exclusive video and audio features. Additionally, it has a growing voice platform, which adds voice messaging to AOL's interactive service.

America Online has more than five thousand employees. You may find job openings in many fields, some of which include account management, animation, content development, finance information technology, and product marketing.

Training and Education. AOL hires interns in most areas of its business. The majority of the opportunities are in their largest sites in Columbus, Ohio, and Mountain View, California, and at the headquarters in northern Virginia. As the company has many people apply for intern positions, AOL has established the following minimum requirements for applications to this program.

- You must be an enrolled college student in good standing.
- You must be eighteen or older at the time of hire.
- You should have a cumulative grade point average of 3.0 or higher.
- You must be available to work a minimum of ten weeks.

Visit the AOL website to learn more about the internship program and career opportunities like those in the following job descriptions. In looking at the full-time jobs, note the diversity of jobs available, and pay special attention to the qualifications needed for the positions that interest you. Most jobs require good communication skills and the ability to work in a team environment.

SAMPLE JOB DESCRIPTIONS

JAVA SOFTWARE ENGINEER

Education Requirement: Bachelor's degree
Professional Experience: Three to five years
Job Description: Develop leading-edge Web applications in a cohesive team environment. Design, develop, debug, and maintain advanced Java applications on a state-of-the-art application server platform in Unix (Solaris). Strong oral and written communication skills. EJ2EE experience including servlets, JSPs and EJBs, HTML, XML, HTTP, application servers, Web servers, and relational databases.

NETWORK TECHNICIAN

Education Requirement: Associate degree/two-year technical school or equivalent experience
Professional Experience: One to two years' related experience
Job Description: Planning and installation of copper, coax, and fiber media. Physical installation and maintenance of LAN media switches/routers and associated line cards. Ability to work independently as well as in a team environment.

BROADBAND DESIGNER

Education Requirement: B.S. or equivalent experience
Professional Experience: Two to four years' related experience
Job Description: This position requires a highly skilled visual artist who has extensive experience as a designer in at least two creative disciplines (graphic design, video, motion graphics, sound design, animation, information architecture).

ASSOCIATE SYSTEM ADMINISTRATOR

Education Requirement: B.S. in computer science or engineering
Professional Experience: Two years' experience in multiplatform environment
Job Description: Installation and setup of servers, monitoring current network infrastructure, troubleshooting, and resolving problems with production systems. HP, SUN, and LINUX experience highly desired. Perl and TCLL scripting a plus.

SPANISH LANGUAGE TRANSLATOR/ANALYST

Education Requirement: Bachelor's degree
Professional Experience: Three or more years of domestic and foreign experience
Job Description: Be part of the Web classification team, building and developing the software that categorizes the content of the Web. Must have strong verbal and excellent written skills in English and either Spanish or Portuguese.

Regional and Local Internet Service Providers

The majority of ISPs are local and regional companies that generally operate in just a few area codes and increasingly offer a high level of customer service and technical support. They range in size from small two- or three-person companies to larger ISPs with one hundred thousand or more customers. The vast majority of these companies offer service in ten or fewer area codes. Their rapid growth reflects the consumer demand for both faster access to the Net and increased customer service.

A Regional ISP Success Story—Jim Deibele and Teleport

In 1987, Jim Deibele owned a bookstore specializing in technical books. Many of his customers often asked him to E-mail them when their special orders arrived. Jim began providing this service from a 386 computer with eight megabytes of RAM (random-access memory) and five hundred megabytes of disk space. In 1989, he upgraded, adding four modems, and began charging five dollars a month—twice the rates of the competition, but Jim advertised that his connections were always available. In 1992, Jim offered his first Internet connection, using a 14.4-speed modem.

Jim's make-or-break year was 1993. His bookstore had folded, and a national ISP had announced its intention to offer Internet access in Portland. Jim worked as a temp to make money to buy better modems for his business. If 1993 was his toughest year, 1994 was his best. Teleport hired its first employee in August, the same day the firm incorporated. Three more were hired later that same year, and in October, Jim was finally able to take a salary for himself and was no longer doing everything, from being the receptionist to handling the billing, but was hiring people who specialized in certain areas.

Teleport became the largest Internet provider in the Northwest, serving Oregon and southwest Washington, with four separate

T-1 lines connecting twenty thousand subscribers. Teleport employed about forty people in a community-oriented business. It offered support and special discounts to teachers, librarians, and nonprofit organizations.

In addition to providing standard consumer access accounts, Teleport also offered virtual server accounts. A virtual server allows you to run your personal website from an ISP's server as if your website had its own dedicated Internet connection. Your website has its own address, as in www.yourname.com. A virtual server account also can provide detailed statistics on which Web pages are being accessed and how often they are accessed. This information can be of great help to a business when making marketing decisions. Before the Internet bubble burst, Teleport was sold to Earthlink, a national company that is looking to acquire even more local and regional service providers.

The Teleport Job Profile. You can learn more about the jobs at a regional Internet service provider by studying the way Teleport was organized as well as the descriptions of technical support and creative services positions. The staff consisted of:

- president and founder
- senior vice president of marketing and communications
- director of operations
- system administration: manager, three operators
- technical support: manager, assistant manager, senior technician, internal support technician, thirteen staff members
- office staff: manager, two receptionists, one staff member
- billing staff: supervisor, two staff members
- creative services: webmaster, art director, designer, researcher, CGI programmer
- outreach: one staff member
- nonprofits coordinator: one staff member
- teleport sales: one staff member

In terms of technical support, most ISPs have a layered system of two or three levels with the most senior staff acting as resource specialists for junior staff. Teleport preferred to hire people with good customer service skills, feeling that it was always possible to train for the technical skills. Creative services personnel generally work for all the customers. Salaries for these positions are not as high as they would be at a marketing or public relations firm.

A Local Internet Service Provider

Cruzio (www.cruzio.com) is one of the oldest and largest network providers in Santa Cruz County, California, offering dial-up, DSL, and ISDN Internet access. It differs from the larger online services in that it offers a community-based, community-oriented connection to the Internet. Cruzio's home page offers links to areas of community information ranging from the media and the arts to weather, tides, and surf. It has information on local events and nine live local Web cameras. Cruzio also has a Web page devoted to "Surfn' Santa Cruz"—the one-stop Web page for all the information you need to plan and enjoy surfing in this beach resort town.

Owners Peggy Dolgenos and Chris Neklason began their careers as software engineers working for a large software company. They had used the Internet and E-mail since the 1980s and felt that these would be useful tools to offer schools and seniors as a community service. They opened Cruzio in 1989, and it took off.

Peggy says that owning a small business is a twenty-four-hour-a-day, seven-day-a-week job. She compares an ISP to a public utility in that service must always be maintained. She is on a pager day and night, as the owner is the end of the line of responsibility and must always be ready to respond to problems—at 5:00 A.M. if necessary. Looking toward the future, she feels that there will always be a niche for the smaller ISP. The Internet is not like TV because with the Net there is actually interaction. People write letters as well as read them. The community ISP is able to meet this need for a higher level of service.

The Future of Local and Regional ISPs

Starting a new Internet service provider business is much more difficult today than when Teleport or Cruzio were launched. People's expectations have changed dramatically over the past few years, and it now takes a substantial amount of money to buy the equipment to provide the necessary level of service. More than 70 percent of the ISPs now offer T-1 lines for voice and data. In the future, there could be between six hundred and six thousand of these local and regional ISPs. The consumer doesn't care who provides the service, just that it is efficient. The smaller-scale ISPs have the advantage of being quicker to realize that what worked yesterday is not going to work tomorrow, whether it is the phone system or the help-desk software. Their engineers are also better able to fine-tune specific locations.

Cable Companies

Many cable companies are poised to take advantage of the surging demand for broadband. Cox Communications, Inc., is the fifth largest cable provider in the United States. It has about twenty thousand employees serving 6.3 million customers. This company looks for individuals with integrity, individuality, ambition, and talent as well as the following traits when hiring:

- **Critical thinking**—seeing the big picture and being analytical; comprehending what you read
- **Communication**—getting your point across effectively when writing and speaking
- **Visionary qualities**—brainstorming, looking to the future, setting goals
- **Self-motivation**—showing a willingness to take the initiative
- **Proficiency with information**—being inquisitive; knowing how to conduct research

- **Global-minded**—understanding and showing an interest in other cultures
- **Team player**—working well with others to achieve common goals

For information about careers in the cable industry, visit the following websites:

Cox Communications	www.cox.com/CoxCareer
Comcast	http://careers.comcast.com

Other Points of Access

Should you decide that you want to help people access the Internet, even more choices await you. An ever-increasing number of options are appearing for accessing the Net.

Area Networks: LAN and WAN

LANs (local-area networks) are limited networks, often owned by businesses and universities, that link computers together with other equipment within a small geographic area. WANs (wide-area networks) connect individual groups with an infrastructure often rented from an Internet service provider. LANs and WANs increasingly are linked to the Internet, although the link may be filtered. This development has created a group of people well versed in Net skills and able to establish Internet links at home.

vBNS—Scientists Network

A very high speed Backbone Network System (vBNS) was opened for scientific use in 1995. Built as a result of a five-year agreement between the National Science Foundation and WorldCom, it supports high-bandwidth, high-performance applications. In 1999 more than one hundred universities and research and education networks were added to vBNS, which began offering commercial service in 2000.

Schools and Libraries

There is increasing determination across the entire nation to see that our schools are connected to the Net. There have been calls for setting aside a portion of the radio frequency spectrum for unlicensed wireless digital communications for schools, libraries, and health-care facilities. This would allow LANs to be established without the necessity of hardwiring buildings. The LANs would in turn connect to the Net. If this new technology can support the higher speed demands of the ever-evolving Internet, then its greatly reduced cost should lead to rapid and widespread adoption and create a demand for both equipment and instructors.

Wi-Fi

Wi-Fi are wireless networks using radio waves to broadcast high-speed Internet access. It currently is available only in the largest cities and is mainly useful to laptop users. It is expected that in the future, networkable PDAs and other portable devices using Wi-Fi technology will become popular. Microsoft has already added a utility that alerts users when they come within range of a Wi-Fi signal.

Internet Telephony

Several services allow people to make phone calls over the Internet rather than over expensive long-distance lines. Other new products allow people to bypass the computer and speak through regular phones over the Internet. Finally, the telephone companies can offer Internet calling as a service, charging an access fee, as they already have an Internet infrastructure in place. Any of these developments open up new employment opportunities.

Future Job Trends—a Note of Caution

With all the enthusiasm over the growth of the Internet, it is important to realize that some of the very developments contributing to the growth of the Net are also causing a decline in certain jobs. Sophisticated software programs have lessened the ISPs' need for large numbers of software engineers. Additionally, the mergers and consolidations of cable and telephone companies, in conjunction with the development of increasingly sophisticated equipment, may lead to an actual decrease in the number of installers and repairers employed by the telephone companies.

For further information on ISPs, look for copies of *Internet World* magazine or visit its website at www.internetworld.com. An E-zine, *LightReading* (www.lightreading.com) is another good information source.

CHAPTER THREE

Providing the Proper Hardware

I f you reduce the Internet to its simplest form, you find that it is composed of three basic parts:

- the individual computer and its associated equipment
- the lines, which are often supplied by a telephone company or increasingly by cable modem
- the hubs, routers, and switches that connect those lines

These parts of the system are called *hardware*. The programs that make the equipment work are called *software*. Those who are actively involved in the design and development of hardware are usually called *hardware engineers*. Assemblers, inspectors, technicians, production staff, product managers, quality control experts, sales and marketing people, education specialists, technical writers, and maintenance people also play key roles in bringing Internet hardware to individuals and companies.

If you are interested in being a part of creating Net hardware, you might work at one of the major equipment vendors, such as Cisco Systems or Nortel Networks, or at a line provider, such as AT&T or SBC. Today's network is composed of equipment that is designed to work together regardless of the manufacturer, using the common standard TCP/IP, which stands for transfer control protocol/Internet protocol. This is called *open architecture* and is partly responsible for the proliferation of manufacturers as well as the rapid development of new technologies.

When each part of a system works with everyone else's part, then a new component of a system can be developed and integrated without having to rebuild the entire system. Small start-up firms are able to get their products to a market that is no longer the exclusive province of the major firms. You may find a job within a large, well-established company or at a small, newly established company.

Hubs, Routers, and Switches

Hubs, routers, and network switches are the devices responsible for moving the Internet traffic to its destination. AOL and other ISPs have had to add routers and other network equipment every eighteen months to service their rapid expansion. The industry involved in building these tools is expected to grow 50 percent in the next year alone. Visit the websites of the top four companies, which together control 85 percent of the industry's revenues and 90 percent of the profits, for information about company and employment opportunities:

Cisco Systems	www.cisco.com
Nortel Networks	www.nortelnetworks.com
3Com	www.3com.com
Enterasys Networks	www.enterasys.com

How They Work

To some degree switches, routers, and hubs all do the same thing, in that they all direct the traffic on the Internet. When you think of switches, think of the telephone companies (Telcos) and local area networks. A router defines a fork in the road based on established rules. Routers sense traffic on a network and route that traffic over a wide-area connection. Additionally, routers talk to each other, continuously sending messages about their current loads.

Hubs are where the wires come together in a central location. Figure 3.1 illustrates how they work together. The cloud in the diagram is a standard depiction of the Internet.

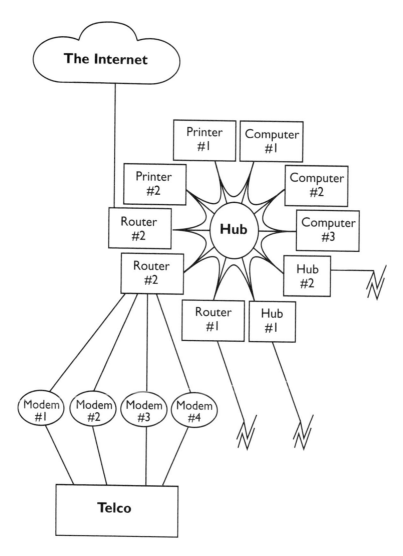

FIGURE 3.1. Hub Diagram

A packet is an amount of data, of a fixed size, encapsulated with addressing and routing information. It is convenient to visualize it as a gel capsule, such as one that might contain aspirin or vitamins. All files are broken up into packets. The number of packets depends on the size of the file. To transmit a file from California to the East Coast, you throw all the packets out into the cloud (the Internet), the switches gobble them up, and the routers send them on their way. Some packets may go through Houston and some through Minneapolis, but they are all reassembled at the destination. If a packet gets lost on the way, the destination point notifies the sender and a replacement packet is transmitted. All of this occurs in a short period of time and is invisible to the user.

A Company Profile: Cisco Systems

Cisco Systems was founded in 1984 by computer scientists from Stanford University who believed that an easier way to connect computer systems was needed. With $18.9 billion in annual revenue in 2002, Cisco Systems has shown the most rapid growth of any company in the high-tech industry. The company's leaders are optimistic about the future and believe that the best of the Internet Revolution is yet to come. Cisco's engineering organization is divided into eleven technology groups: IOS Technologies, Internet Switching and Services, Core Routing, Network Management Services, Optical, Storage, Voice, Aggregation, Access, Ethernet Access, and Wireless.

Cicso hires highly talented people, usually the top ten percent of job seekers. Most jobs require a master's degree or equivalent in an engineering/technical discipline. The company is looking for people who are detail oriented with good communication skills and the ability to work in a team environment. For current information on available jobs, check Cisco's website at www.cisco.com.

Cisco's Certification Program. Many makers of hardware offer training and certification programs in using their technologies. Industry standard certifications are often required for positions working with advanced technologies. Obtianing such certifications can enhance your career opportunities.

Cisco sponsors the Networking Academy Program, which began in 1997 as a high school network support curriculum and has since evolved into a global educational program with 260,000 students enrolled at 9,800 academies. It offers online instructor-led training and hands-on laboratory exercises and currently has the following courses: CCNA, which offers a basic foundation in networking; CCNP, which develops more advanced network skills; PC Hardware and Software, sponsored by Hewlett-Packard; Network Operating Systems, also sponsored by HP; Fundamentals of Java Programming, sponsored by Sun Microsystems; Fundamentals of Network Security; Fundamentals of UNIX, sponsored by Sun Microsystems; Fundamentals of Voice and Data Cabling, sponsored by Panduit; and Fundamentals of Web Design, sponsored by Adobe Systems.

Click on "Success Stories" on the Net Academy home page (http://cisco.netacad.net) for interesting stories about students from around the world. Also, click on "Workforce Development" to see the job placement program, which links academy students and alumni with employers.

Making the Connection: The Lines

Faster is better, and to a major extent the speed of your Internet connection is determined by the type of line you use. Most consumers connect to an ISP using POTS (plain old telephone service) through a 56 kbps modem. A faster connection for the home or small business user is an ISDN (integrated services digital network) line at 128 kbps. Both POTS and ISDN are on-demand lines, which means you are not connected to the Net until you sign on. Many companies use lines that are dedicated and operate at 128 kbps. A switched line has dial-up service (you only pay for what you use), while a dedicated line is always connected to the Internet and is used by companies needing full-time access. A T-1 line is the backbone of the telephone infrastructure. It offers a direct connection to the Internet and is frequently used to connect local-area networks. A T-3 line carries twenty-eight times the capacity of a T-1 line and is used mainly by business customers needing ultrafast data or video transmission.

Broadband

While more than seventy-five million households live in areas with access to broadband, only fifteen million currently have connections through digital subscriber lines (DSLs) or cable modems. *Broadband* generally refers to a wide band of frequencies, which allows information to be sent on many different channels at the same time.

Although the switch to broadband is still just beginning, the potential looks enormous. While an always-on connection and faster downloads are enticements, the real excitement is in the potential for new technologies, such as being able to download feature films. Already special programs are in existence for these rapid connections. AOL offers subscribers a special-content package with videos and music. ABC News on Demand offers large sections of its daily broadcasts. Microsoft has Xbox Live, which allows gamers to compete on the Internet. Additionally, broadband stands to help small and medium-sized businesses that could not otherwise afford the dedicated T-1 lines.

Integrated Services Digital Network (ISDN)

The high cost of direct T-1 connections to the Internet puts them beyond the reach of most individuals. ISDN lines are a partial solution. They upgrade today's standard analog telephone network to a digital system. With the exception of the part running from the local exchange to your office or home, the world's telephone network is already digital. ISDN upgrades that final link of the system. With ISDN, you can be online and talk on the phone over the same line at the same time. ISDN operates at speeds up to 128 kbps. It is especially helpful in speeding up the transfer of rich media, graphics, and audio and visual applications. It is available in most urban and suburban areas.

Asymmetric Digital Subscriber Line (ADSL) and Cable Modems

ADSL is asymmetric in that you are able to receive a lot more data than with an ISDN line but you are limited in the amount you can send back. ADSL and cable modems both offer 512 kbps of bandwidth and use existing lines or cables. The greater bandwidth is important for developing markets offering information in multimedia and video formats. ADSL has just reached one million customers in North America. Even faster lines, such as very high speed digital subscriber lines (VDSL), are being planned by the telephone companies, but they are being challenged by cable television and wireless methods, including cellular, microwave, and satellite.

Wireless

Telephone companies are interested in a new technology called EvDo, short for Evolution Data Only, which can provide wireless connections ten times faster than a regular modem. It is faster than the wireless WiFi connections and can work over existing cell phone networks. You would be able to connect to the Internet from anywhere you get a mobile phone signal.

For further information on high-speed lines, check the following websites:

National ISDN Council	www.nationalisdncouncil.com
DSL Forum	www.dslforum.org
Broadband Daily	www.broadband-daily.com
CED magazine	www.cedmagazine.com

Working with ISDN

William Moore describes himself as a software guy gone bad. With a degree in computer science from the University of California at San Diego, he now works for a major telephone company as a second-level manager in data products. He works with ISDN in market and channel development brand management, handling his company's ISDN website. Although he oversees the program, he contracts with outside firms to provide employees to work on specific areas of his website, such as the back-end database. William says the value of the Web is "just smoking," particularly for advertising and electronic commerce. A good website can often make things easier for customers to find the information they want, thus generating higher customer satisfaction. William tries to work with the attitude: "What can I do today to make a significant impact?"

Working with Other Types of Hardware

While the Internet already has made a major impact on our society, its potential for future change and growth remains enormous. Hardware is continuously being created and modified as developments in technology offer new choices. Imagine being a part of developing some of the new Net hardware that we will be seeing in the next ten years.

These are exciting times for those of you who want jobs that will change the face of the Internet as we know it. In the future, many consumer products will be connected to the Internet, from televisions to digital cameras, mobile phones, and PDAs. Video-on-demand is expected to become the most popular service of the cable operators. Home networking is expected to take off as more and more homes have several PCs. The Web on TV has arrived via an Internet appliance that is simple to use and is half the size of a VCR. In the works is a stripped-down dedicated computer that will allow you to surf the Web and get E-mail while storing your files on your ISP's computer. Wireless Internet access for your notebook computer is now available.

BlackBerry handhelds offer completely embedded wireless technology. They are designed to provide a secure and continuous connection to the wireless network. It is expected that this type of technology will be adopted by most wireless devices, from phones to PDAs. How about a cordless Internet controller, allowing you to sit back in comfort when surfing the Web? Good news for couch potatoes. Sound cards and video cards are becoming increasingly sophisticated to take advantage of the multimedia offered on the Web. The top monitors are able to display brighter colors and better contrast and handle graphics easily. The Internet is on a continuous cycle where each advance in programs and services stimulates a demand for increased speed, and each advance in speed opens up a new area of possible services. The market for people to design and build Internet hardware will be strong for the foreseeable future, although just which line or piece of hardware will be the standard in the future is still to be determined.

Running an Intranet

Don Jensen keeps 110 people at Granite Construction Company connected to the Internet. He runs an intranet, a private internal resource that connects to a national ISP offering dedicated connections of 56 kbps, which are each one-twenty-fourth of a T-1 connection. The company's main hub is located in Watsonville, California, and the others are in Dallas, Atlanta, and Tampa.

Each of the company's 110 employees has his or her own Internet address. While an ISP with ten subscribers per modem is generally considered to offer good service, Don has arranged for the company to have almost a one-to-one ratio, as many of the employees are online all day. Granite Construction Company also has a toll-free number so that workers who are traveling can easily plug in their laptops from a hotel room.

Don is responsible for installing and maintaining all the equipment as well as for training the personnel in the use of the Internet. By connecting people to the home office using the Internet, Don has saved the company hundreds of thousands of dollars in long-distance telephone bills. His work hours are long when he is out of the main office. On the road, Don frequently works at night because the company offices are so busy during the day. The most interesting part of his job, Don finds, is giving a system to a new user who has only heard about the Internet and never used it. The Net neophyte usually can't believe the speed of communication and data links available on the Internet.

Don points out that if you work with hardware, you must keep up with the technology or you'll quickly find your job skills obsolete. The Internet is like a moving river—you need to swim with it and realize that it is going to be different every year. For this reason, it is very important for employees in this area to be the type who welcome change. In Don's field, equipment will become easier to run; however, there will always be a need for someone to take the computer, put it on someone's desk, and teach him or her how to run it.

Don sees a chasm developing between the computer scientist and the Internet technician. As each occupation has become vastly more complex over the last few years, the two no longer communicate well with each other in many cases. Don feels that the best preparation for an information technology career today is a four-year degree along with a very wide range of certifications.

A Career in Hardware: Sample Jobs

Here is a close look at several jobs in the hardware industry.

Electronic Engineers

Electronic engineers design, develop, test, and supervise the manufacture of electronic equipment. They also write performance requirements and develop maintenance schedules. A bachelor's degree is usually required for these positions, with many job applicants having master's degrees. Pay starts at more than $40,000 per year, with the median pay for midlevel engineers at about $67,000. Engineers at senior managerial levels receive a median salary of approximately $130,000. With the rapid expansion of the Internet, college graduates with knowledge of the latest technologies will continue to be in demand.

Systems Analysts

LANs (local-area networks) and WANs (wide-area networks) are frequently designed by systems analysts who use their knowledge and skills in a problem-solving capacity. They may design entirely new systems, combining hardware and software to allow for the free exchange of data. A growing number of systems analysts are employed on a temporary or contract basis or as consultants. A bachelor's degree in a computer-related field is almost always required. Median annual earnings of computer systems analysts are close to $60,000. There is a continued demand by businesses for networking systems, which should ensure job opportunities for applicants whose skills are current.

Electronic Engineering Technicians

Electronic engineering technicians use knowledge of electronic circuits to design, develop, and manufacture electronic equipment. Many technicians assist engineers and scientists, especially in research and development. Prospective engineering technicians should take as many high school science and math courses as possible. Advanced training is required by most employers and is available at technical institutes, community colleges, and extension divisions of four-year colleges and universities. Many employers emphasize the need for good communication skills and the ability to work with others as technicians often work as part of a team. Beginning salaries average more than $25,000 a year.

Those in senior or supervisory positions earn close to $60,000. While technicians will remain in demand, the growing availability and use of advanced technologies is expected to curtail employment growth in this field.

Equipment Operators

As more and more establishments realize the need to connect all their computers in LANs in order to enhance productivity, there will be an increasing demand for full-time operators. Sophisticated computer programs now enable the computer to perform many routine tasks formerly done by computer operators, whose attention now will be directed toward troubleshooting, technical assistance, system security, network problems, and maintenance of large databases. Previous work experience and computer-related training, perhaps through a community college or industry certification program, are job requirements in many large establishments. Full-time computer operators have median earnings of close to $28,000 a year, with the lowest 10 percent earning below $20,000 and the top 10 percent earning above $40,000 per year.

Data Processing Equipment Repairers

Data processing equipment repairers are also called service technicians or field service representatives. They install, maintain, and repair electronic equipment. As the number of computers in service increases, so will the demand for people to repair them. Median annual earnings of full-time data processing equipment repairers are close to $30,000.

Developing Your Own Career in Hardware

If you are seriously thinking about a career in the Internet industry, you must keep track of current trends in order to make solid career decisions. Competition is so fierce and innovation so rapid in this industry that giant firms can stumble, and newcomers can rapidly disappear. Furthermore, much of your value to your employer will depend on your knowledge of the latest technologies in the hardware field. You will need to continue your education throughout your career.

One possible job avenue to consider is working abroad. A great number of jobs are going to open up in other countries. The pioneer spirit has greatly influenced the development of the Internet in the United States. Companies have been willing to invest a lot of money simply on faith, a model that works well in this country. Businesses in many foreign countries have felt the need to quantify the value of every undertaking and have been slower to hop aboard the Net bandwagon. Eventually, they will need help in adopting the new technologies or risk being left behind.

CHAPTER FOUR

Software: Making the Hardware Work

Whatever you do online—whether it is sending E-mail to a friend, buying a bicycle or a book, accessing a website, or downloading a file—a software program is involved. Software programs are what make Internet and computer equipment work. Visit any bricks-and-mortar or online store selling software, and you will see the vast number of programs that have been created for business, pleasure, and education.

Careers in Software

Many individuals are involved in developing software. There are careers in software for developers, salespeople, marketers, advertisers, teachers, trainers, writers, managers, and researchers. Here is a look at what some of these professionals do.

- **Computer software engineers** are responsible for the design, development, testing, and evaluation of the software that makes computers work. While software engineers must be good programmers, they are more concerned with solving programming problems than with actually writing code.
- **Applications software engineers** analyze users' needs and create, design, or modify applications software.
- **Systems software engineers** construct and maintain a company's computer systems and plan their future growth.

- **Systems analysts** work with an organization to solve computer problems and enable computer technology to best serve that organization. Systems analysts are also called *systems developers* or *systems architects*.
- **Computer scientists** work as theorists, researchers, or inventors. They may work in academic institutions as well as in private industry.
- **Database administrators** use software to organize and store data. They are often responsible for planning and coordinating security measures.
- **Computer programmers** write, test, and maintain the detailed instructions, called programs, that computers must follow in order to work.
- **Applications programmers** write programs to handle a specific job within an organization, such as inventory tracking.
- **Systems programmers** write programs to maintain and control computer systems software, such as operating systems, networked systems, and database systems.

Internet Software Developments

Software developments are in large part responsible for the directions in which the Internet has grown. The Internet is made up of many different kinds of computers, from PCs to mainframes. TCP/IP (transfer control protocol/Internet protocol) is a system of protocols used by all computers that allows them to talk to each other. A protocol is a set of instructions used by computers to describe how information is shared between them. Without a universal system like TCP/IP, computers could not communicate with each other and there would be no Internet. Many Net software programs are based on TCP/IP, such as FTP (file transfer protocol), Telnet, and World Wide Web (WWW) browsers.

E-Mail Programs

E-mail was one of the first services developed for the Internet. Originally designed to exchange information, it has become an extraordinarily popular method for personal communication. It is also being increasingly used in business to allow clients to report problems and request information about services and products. Some of the most widely used E-mail programs are Eudora (www.eudora.com), Microsoft Outlook, and Outlook Express (www.microsoft.com). More information about E-mail software may be found at the programs' websites.

HTML: Web Page Language

HTML (hypertext markup language) is a universal language used to create Web pages. It allows a document to be correctly displayed on any screen regardless of the type of computer or terminal being used. Hypertext contains links to other documents embedded within the text. It allows users to quickly access related text from within the document they are reading. Hypermedia documents contain not just text but pictures, graphics, sounds, and even animation. Dedicated HTML authoring tools include Adobe GoLive (www.adobe.com/products/golive), Microsoft FrontPage (www.microsoft.com/frontpage), and Macromedia's Dreamweaver (www.macromedia.com).

Web Browsers: Surfing the Net

The development of Web browser programs led to the great surge in popularity of Web surfing by providing a simple way to navigate the Web. An important aspect of the browser is the ease with which it can be extended to add players for sound, viewers for graphic files, and what seems to be an unending list of exciting new applications for various purposes. The line between the Internet and the Web is increasingly blurred as more and more Internet tools (software programs) are added to browsers. Two of the major browsers are Netscape's Navigator (www.netscape.com) and Microsoft's Internet Explorer (www.microsoft.com). Both companies are actively adding new personnel to support their growth and to help them extend their range of services. They also list job offerings on their Web pages.

Search Engines: Finding Information

The Internet is growing so fast and in so many different directions at once that any attempt to list its resources is doomed to failure. Search engines, using the Web browser interface, allow Web users to find the information they seek, whether it is a company that sells teddy bears or a government document. Many commercial search engines make the research job easier by offering reviews and commentary. Popular commercial search engines include:

Google	www.google.com
MSN Search	www.search.msn.com
Ask Jeeves	www.askjeeves.com
Yahoo!	www.yahoo.com
Lycos	www.lycos.com
WebCrawler	www.webcrawler.com

A Company Profile: Google

The name Google was inspired by the term *googol,* which refers to the numeral 1 followed by one hundred zeros. This huge number represents the company's desire to organize the incredible amount of information available on the Web. Larry Page and Sergey Brin were graduate students at Stanford University in 1996 when they began working together on a search engine that could analyze the "back links" to a website. By 1998 they had set up Google's first data center in Larry's dorm room. When they were unable to interest the portal companies in their technology, they decided to build their own company. After raising almost $1 million, their business opened in a garage rented from a friend with a total staff of three. By early 1999 they had moved into an office in Palo Alto, had eight employees, and Google was answering half a million queries per day. Quickly outgrowing this office, they moved to their current headquarters in Mountain View, California, which they named the Googleplex.

While developing their software, they also developed a unique company culture. Rubber exercise balls doubled as mobile office chairs, lava lamps proliferated, and large dogs roamed the halls. A chef was hired based on his health-conscious recipes, and roller hockey games were held in the parking lot twice a week. This informality helped develop good working relationships among the staff and led to rapid exchanges of ideas.

By the middle of 2000, Google was a solid business answering eighteen million user queries a day. On June 26, 2000, Google announced a partnership with Yahoo!, which was followed by many other partnerships. The Google Toolbar was launched in late 2000. By the fourth quarter of 2001, Google was showing a profit. The company currently has more than five hundred employees, more than fifty with doctorate degrees. Together, their employees speak thirty-four languages.

Google Job Opportunities

At the time of writing, Google was offering jobs in the following departments: Engineering and Operations, Sales and Field Operations, Product Management, Corporate Communications, Legal, Marketing, Finance, Facilities, International, and Human Resources. There are many possible job opportunities for you at Google. Some of them are outlined here.

Summer Interns. Google offers a summer internship program for students currently enrolled in Ph.D. or M.S. programs in computer science. To qualify for the job, you should have extensive experience in systems software or algorithms, excellent skills in C++ and Python, and knowledge of UNIX/Linux or Windows environments as well as familiarity with TCP/IP and network programming.

Software Engineers. Google looks for software engineers to develop the next generation search engine. The company wants people with "a need to bring order to a chaotic Web." For this job, you need a B.S. or M.S. in computer science as well as several years of experience in software development. You should have solid knowledge of and experience in the following areas: C++, Unix/Linux or Windows operating environments, TCP/IP, and network programming.

Software Engineers (Java). Google hires Java software engineers to write server-side code for Web-based applications. It also wants well-rounded developers who can create strong production applications. To qualify, you need a B.S. or M.S. in computer science or equivalent, strong skills in Java, experience using SQL, some database design experience, development experience in a Unix/Linux environment, and the ability to use Python and C++.

Software Engineers (Windows). Google needs Windows developers to design and develop cutting-edge search tools. Google wants people with "a passion for driving and building new technologies," as well as the ability to work in a small team. You need a B.S. or M.S. in computer science or equivalent, extensive experience programming in C/C++/COM, OO skills; and extensive knowledge of Windows SDK and Win32 API. It would be helpful to have experience in user-interface development, multi-threaded software, Windows NT security, and network protocols.

A Programmer at a Large Company

Owen Hill works as a programmer for SBC. Although he received his undergraduate degree in finance and an M.B.A. in international business, Owen was trained by SBC as a programmer and has taken extensive training in client server application development. Owen supports an established SBC client server application and has assisted a project that mechanized a testing process using Java, Python, C++, VB 4.0, and other development tools.

Owen and his team use the Internet to stay current with technology as it relates to the software tools they use. This technology can change on a daily if not hourly basis. He feels that the Internet is the primary source for this information because it is constantly available and can be focused specifically on his needs. Newsgroups, chat rooms, and MSDN also offer effective ways to gain support from experienced users. Owen reports that there are simply not enough students coming out of schools with a background in client server development tools and concepts.

The Future in Programming

In the future, Owen sees companies like his focusing more and more on core technologies. In an economy increasingly based on the "knowledge worker," this focus will increase the number of job opportunities for outside suppliers and their teams of contractors. Such contractors currently earn between $45 and $60 per hour, depending on their experience. Consultants can earn $50 to $150 per hour providing what is little more than proper project management of an application or website development.

Network support requirements in the future will be huge. Owen sees an ongoing demand for electrical engineers, network designers, and server administrators. Database administrators, low-level programmers (they get down to the bits and bytes using languages such as C++), and help desk support will be needed, as will trainers in all categories for both software and hardware.

Developing New Technologies

Michael Killianey is a software engineer who worked on developing WebTV. The software he wrote resides inside a box that connects a TV to the Internet. The box is basically an Internet browser that is also capable of offering E-mail and other services. He both wrote the code and worked on upgrades to the system. He found it exciting that his company was virtually unknown and in six months became the de facto industry leader.

When Michael first started working for WebTV, it was a small firm with only twenty or thirty employees. Everyone worked closely together and did a little bit of everything. After the company grew to nearly two hundred employees, everyone had a more precise job description. Michael found that with thirty or forty people who do similar things, the opportunity to learn from each other is greater.

Michael has a liberal arts degree in an interdisciplinary major and a master's degree in computer science. He paid for his education by teaching computer science classes and tutoring students in math, which he calls "a beautiful discipline." His first job was with an artificial intelligence firm doing work for the government. It only lasted three weeks. He found he was working an exact forty-hour week and having to account for his time in fifteen-minute increments. At WebTV Michael came to work whenever he felt ready to be productive, at 8:00 A.M. one day and 11:00 A.M. the next. He notes that you can't always think of a creative way to solve a problem at work; you may be at home cooking dinner when an idea strikes. What's important is not the number of hours, but the amount of work you get done.

After his government job, Michael developed video games for Rocket Science Games. He worked on full-motion video, which gives an experience similar to watching a movie and playing a video game at the same time. He then worked for WebTV for several years until it was bought by MSN.

Michael finds that, at its best, writing software allows one to create amazingly powerful solutions. He explains that when a civil engineer designs a road system, that solution is local and specific to the area. In contrast, a well-designed software solution is often generic and can be used again and again with few changes. The challenge of the Internet is that the content is always changing and new standards are continually emerging. The release of a software upgrade can be awaited with the same excitement as the release of a new movie.

According to Michael, software design is big business in which the best man doesn't always win. Software is in itself an abstract commodity, just a series of ones and zeros. Its value is determined by what becomes the industry standard. There are many adequate solutions in the rush to develop technology, but it is the solution that is accepted that accrues the value.

A Self-Employed Programmer

John Buckman ran a small Internet software company from his home. He wrote and sold software for running E-mail discussion groups on the Internet. He has written a program, TILE, which converts Lotus Notes databases to HTML and which attracted a number of major customers. TILE allows users to easily create websites from databases. It also allows users to browse the database by any number of categories. TILE is now part of the List-Universe.com Network, which has more than thirty websites, fifty newsletters, and six moderated discussion lists serving E-mail list owners and E-zine publishing professionals.

John started working when he was fourteen as an intern at Yale University doing menial computer work. He moved up to being a programmer at the Yale University HMO during high school and college summers. He got a bachelor's degree in philosophy from Bates College and a master's in philosophy from the Sorbonne. After college, he went to work at a "futures-oriented think tank" for a year and then spent a year as a general computer consultant with a small consulting firm. After one and a half years as a programmer at the Discovery Channel, he started his own company and has been self-employed ever since.

After working on his own for several years, John says that he can never go back to working for someone else. He works seven days a week, typically from 9:00 A.M. to 11:00 P.M. with about three hours of break time during the day. Mostly he programs, although he also talks to clients over the telephone and very occasionally gives sales presentations. He spends about three hours a day answering E-mail.

John finds that self-pacing is both extremely difficult and extremely important. The challenges are mostly psychological in that it is easy to get depressed when things are not going well, and this can allow you to fall into a self-defeating slump. John initially had a difficult time with the traditional business aspects—such as accounts receivable, contracts, and taxes—but he notes that these things tend to sort themselves out over time.

John says that he sees a lot of shoddy work on the Internet, even from big companies. He believes that this presents a great opportunity for talented entrepreneurs who do quality work because they can effectively compete with huge companies, and the potential payoffs are great. The one recommendation he makes is never to show poor-quality work to the public. Because the Internet is so intangible, all that people have to base their opinions on is the quality of your work. Make sure that everything the public sees is top-notch. If you're not a graphic designer, don't do your own website; find a talented friend to do it for you.

Job Outlooks in Software Development

Computer software engineering is expected to be the fastest-growing occupation over the next few years. You should have at least a bachelor's degree in computer science or engineering as well as practical work experience. Strong problem-solving and analytical skills are required if you wish to become a software engineer. Additionally, you should be able to communicate effectively with both team members and customers.

Starting salary offers are more than $50,000 for those with bachelor's degrees and around $60,000 for those with master's degrees.

Systems analysts, computer scientists, and database administrators are also projected to be among the fastest-growing occupations. While many positions require a bachelor's degree, there are some that require only a two-year degree. Programs offered by community colleges and independent technical institutes may be geared toward local businesses and are often more occupation specific than a four-year curriculum. Regardless of degree, relevant work experience is very important. Starting offers for graduates with bachelor's degrees average close to $52,000 in computer science and $46,000 in computer systems analysis and in management information systems. Starting salaries for database administrators can range from $72,000 to more than $100,000.

Employment of computer programmers is expected to grow much more slowly than that of other computer specialists. Sophisticated computer software is now capable of writing basic code, eliminating the need for programmers to do this. Additionally, there is increasing competition from overseas businesses that can contract routine work at lower cost. As a programmer, you would frequently be employed on a temporary or contract basis or work as an independent consultant.

Job prospects are best for those with good working knowledge of programming languages such as C, C++, and Java, as well as newer, domain-specific languages. Becoming certified can give you a competitive edge. As in every career field related to the rapidly evolving Internet, it is of paramount importance that programmers remain up-to-date on the latest developments in this dynamic field.

CHAPTER FIVE

Making the Net Accessible for Companies

I t has become almost a requirement for a company to have an Internet presence. Some companies want to advertise, market, or sell their products and services using this powerful medium. Other companies put information about their companies online to attract investors and customers and to describe employment opportunities. Whatever the reason, this avalanche of companies coming aboard the Net means jobs for cybersurfers who can help the companies become active players on the Internet. In addition to jobs in more technical areas, such as providing the necessary hardware, software, and programming discussed in the preceding two chapters, there are jobs in marketing, advertising, sales, and consulting. These jobs are being filled by company employees and by independent contractors and consultants.

Internet Presence Providers

Both large and small businesses often use the services of Internet presence providers (IPPs). An IPP can design, host, and maintain a website. At its simplest, a website is a collection of files residing on a computer called a Web server that is connected to the Internet. Hosting encompasses providing space on a server and Internet access connections—some of which can be quite powerful. Maintenance includes the full-time supervision of the server, software, and hardware as well as the monitoring of the number of "hits" (times that the website is visited). In addition, IPPs offer the necessary technical help to build websites and the marketing and advertising savvy to promote the business on the Net. They also assist companies in registering domain names with the Internet Network Information Center, or InterNIC (www.internic.net), a data and directory service. IPPs are often used by companies that require a national presence for a website with a fairly large amount of traffic yet do not want to dedicate their resources to maintaining a full in-house staff. Large companies provide these services in all-inclusive packages, while regional companies and independent contractors and consultants may concentrate on providing just one service or a limited number of services.

An Internet Presence Provider: Verio

Incorporated in 1996, Verio is the world's largest Web-hosting company. It has a local presence in the major metropolitan areas in the United States and provides services to customers in more than 170 countries. Verio offers dedicated Internet access with lines ranging from a T-1 at 1.54 Mbps to an OC12 at 622 Mbps. Its site supports most website design and publishing tools and also offers technical support and E-commerce applications, which allow users to build and operate Web stores. Check the Verio website at www.verio.com for jobs similar to those described below.

Broadband Technical Support Representative. This individual provides technical assistance and customer service in a call center–type environment and must be available to work a variety of hours. A college degree or equivalent experience, excellent customer service skills, and strong troubleshooting expertise are required. An understanding of Microsoft Office applications and Windows operating systems as well as a strong familiarity with E-mail protocols and clients are needed. A knowledge of Web-based applications, DNS, FTP, and Telnet is required, and certifications such as CCNA and MCSE are a plus.

Wintel Engineer. This engineer works with customers to translate their needs into detailed technical requirements and then configures and tests the hardware and software to assure product performance. Explicit hands-on technical experience and practical knowledge of the Windows NT/2000 environment, file system (DOS and NTFS), networking components, and different tunable registry and network parameters are needed. The ability to resolve integration conflicts between databases, applications, and online libraries is also a must.

Web Hosts

Small and medium-sized businesses often use the services of a Web host. In this area, Interland is the number one Web-hosting company. It began in Boise, Idaho, in 1995 as Micron Electronics but in 2001 sold all its nonhosting business assets, changed the company name, and moved the headquarters to Atlanta, Georgia. The company now offers a wide variety of standardized business-class Web-hosting, E-commerce, and application-hosting services and expects the Web-hosting market as a whole to grow at an annual compound rate of 33.4 percent, reaching more than $16 billion by 2005. While companies with fewer than a thousand employees represent 90 percent of the market, only 17 percent of them have serious websites. The growth potential seems enormous. Check out the Interland website at www.interland.com, where you might find jobs similar to the following.

DESKTOP SUPPORT ADMINISTRATOR

Job Description: Diagnose, troubleshoot, and repair errors with software, hardware, and network connectivity on end-user workstations.

Qualifications: At least one year's experience in a corporate help-desk environment and must be adept at using and troubleshooting all Microsoft Office applications and Internet Explorer. Certifications such as A+, MCSA, or MCSE are helpful.

MARKETING SPECIALIST

Job Description: Writing, editing, and proofing website content, customer communications, newsletter articles, E-mail, and sales collateral and proposals.

Qualifications: Bachelor's degree in marketing, business, or a similar field and two years' professional copywriting experience. High-tech experience is preferred. Must be proficient in Microsoft Word and PowerPoint, with a working knowledge of Microsoft Excel.

Website Design Services

Instead of using an Internet presence provider or Web host, companies can have their websites designed by a professional design firm or by one of the thousands of individual Web designers offering this service. Companies then use an Internet service provider to host their sites. Most large ISPs offer hosting services. For businesses that want to go it alone, a variety of tools are available. Software such as Macromedia's Dreamweaver (www.macromedia .com/software/dreamweaver) and the popular Microsoft Front-Page (www.microsoft.com/frontpage) by are designed to make it easier to program in HTML for the company or individual building a website.

Online Malls

Online malls, or cybermalls, are electronic versions of bricks-and-mortar shopping malls. The malls host websites for merchants, provide the equipment and phone lines they need, and offer marketing, site maintenance, and security. The merchants may pay a monthly rental fee or a percentage of their sales to the mall owner for the privilege of having a store at the mall. Just like land-based malls, cybermalls often are based around a large department store that is the initial draw for attracting customers. Internet mall shoppers are generally an upscale clientele who tend to make purchase decisions quickly. As malls have achieved the ability to offer secure ordering services through credit-card encryption, they are now growing to their full potential. Cybermalls need technical, marketing, sales, and business professionals to set up and promote the mall stores.

Dave Taylor and the Internet Mall

In 1994, Dave Taylor turned an online hobby into the Internet Mall, the first online shopping directory. He was able to raise over $1 million in venture funding, eventually selling the business to TechWave.

Dave is a very knowledgeable cybersurfer. He has a bachelor's degree in computer science and a master's in educational computing and is working on a master's in business administration. He has written several books, including *Learning Mac OS X* and *Teach Yourself Unix System Administration in 24 Hours*. While building his cybermall, Dave also spent time on his consulting company, Intuitive Systems (www.intuitive.com). His principal challenge was to get things out and working in "Internet time" while still having the appearance of a life. Dave sees the Internet as a great liberator intellectually because suddenly things can be created and brought online very quickly. He says the problem, of course, is that because it can be done quickly, suddenly it must be done quickly, and that's anathema to quality and careful design.

Career Advice from Dave. Dave states that it is important to realize that the people with successful online careers are those who have good communication skills. He believes that there is really no substitute for good reading and writing ability. Writing is equally important as reading because whether you're designing a Web page, adding your two cents' worth to an online discussion, or programming a Java applet, it's all about communication between you and your intended audience.

Careers in Marketing and Advertising

Marketing and advertising managers work together to promote a firm's products and services. Part of this promotion is now being done on the Internet; individuals with expertise in this new field are finding jobs with marketing and advertising firms and as consultants.

Marketing managers determine the demand for a company's products and services and identify potential consumers. These managers develop pricing strategies, monitor trends that indicate the need for new products and services, and oversee product development. Advertising managers oversee the account services, creative services, and media services departments. Marketing and advertising managers often work long hours, including evenings and weekends. Working under pressure is unavoidable as schedules change, problems arise, and deadlines and goals must be met.

Salaries start at about $28,000 for advertising managers and $36,000 for marketing managers. Experienced managers earn more than $70,000, while the top 10 percent of managers earns more than $130,000. Surveys show that salary levels vary substantially, depending upon the level of managerial responsibility, length of service, and the size and location of the employer.

An Interactive Marketing Manager

Marvin Chow is the interactive marketing manager at Reebok International. He is responsible for all of the interactive ventures of the brand, including website and online development strategy, CD-ROM production, and digital kiosk work. He uses the Internet for research, content and development ideas, and references. Marvin, who has a bachelor's degree in marketing and computer science, believes that the following skills and abilities are necessary in order to be a good marketing manager:

- technical and marketing background and understanding
- skills to oversee project development
- ability to communicate the creative visions of the brand
- ability to convey technical innovations and possibilities to those of a nontechnical background
- ability to interact with people from all backgrounds
- visionary attitude about the future of this new technology

Marketing and the Internet. Marvin believes that the Internet breathes life into many senior marketing professionals because of its communication capabilities and global reach. It is this ability to deliver energy and enthusiasm to the profession that Marvin enjoys most about his work. The downsides of his job include long hours (anywhere from sixty to ninety hours a week), occasional frustration in explaining the technicalities of the Net, and a lack of recognition by those who don't understand the new medium.

Marvin believes that the Internet will evolve into a total marketing medium similar to print or broadcast. The interactive and online media will begin to integrate into the marketing mix along with public relations, advertising, and retail merchandising. With the emergence of fully integral advertising agencies, the need for interactive managers, like Marvin, will become more critical.

An Expert in Online Marketing Solutions

Before Daniel Janal launched his career as an Internet consultant, he was an award-winning newspaper reporter and business news editor and had worked in public relations. His main job today is to advise clients on how to market on the Net. Through his experience in public relations, he definitely knows what works and what does not. He finds that many companies have unrealistic expectations about the ways in which Net marketing can help their businesses. Daniel gives them options about what to do when they don't know what to do.

His firm, Janal Communications, works with clients from Reader's Digest to small mom-and-pop operations that want to reach online audiences. This may involve designing an online contest, publicizing a website, doing market research, doing competitive analysis, or planning and creating marketing materials. Daniel typically works with his clients and then goes on the Internet to do research. In the future, he believes companies will spend more time on marketing than on the technical aspects of the Internet.

Internet Consultants

Eventually, every company is likely to have an online presence and to use that presence in some way to market a product or service. Many companies use consultants to help them gain a presence on the Internet and to use the Net wisely. Sometimes, these consultants help choose the companies or individuals that a firm needs to get online. At other times, they may perform specific tasks that employees do not have the time or expertise to handle.

Obviously, consultants have to be Net savvy; they may also need to have strong technical, financial, business, marketing, library, or advertising skills. There are literally thousands of Internet consultants working with clients in one-time or long-term relationships. How much consultants earn depends upon their skills as well as their ability to find clients. Some earn as much as $125,000 a year or more.

An Internet Consultant's Story

Margaret Riley Dikel brings her expertise as a librarian, webmaster, and creator of *The Riley Guide* (an online job resources guide described in Chapter 1) to her work as an Internet consultant specializing in employment and recruiting services online. While working as a circulation/computer resources librarian, her reputation as an expert in online job searching began to grow as she built a solid following of career counselors. Soon she was being asked to do outside seminars and got a lot of speaking engagements. When outside work began to conflict more and more with her job as a librarian, she decided to take her chances and become a consultant.

Margaret consults to the career services industry, creating Internet resource libraries and assisting with the navigational design of sites focused on aiding in the job search and online information retrieval processes. Margaret also spends a tremendous amount of time doing presentations for career counselors and job search counselors on using the Internet. She does not work with job seekers but concentrates on working with the counselors and trainers who work with them. In order to provide her clients with the services they require, Margaret can spend up to six hours a day online, looking at employment and recruiting services and evaluating them—an appealing task for a cybersurfer.

Requisite Skills. In order to handle her job as a consultant, Margaret believes that the abilities to teach, to present information in a way that is easy for all users to understand, to create a flow of information that is logical, and to negotiate between systems developers and programmers and users are fundamental. She also feels that it is essential for consultants to be enthusiastic about their work.

Computer Support Specialists

There is a growing need for computer support specialists to provide technical assistance, support, and advice to customers and other users of online websites. Computer support specialists are expected to be among the fastest growing occupations in the next ten years. Job prospects are best for college graduates who are up-to-date with the latest skills and technologies. Certifications and practical experience are essential for persons without degrees. Because of the explosive demand for specialists, relevant computer experience in some cases may substitute for formal education. Job promotions usually depend more on performance than on formal education. Starting salaries range from $30,000 to more than $50,000 for help-desk staff and from $48,000 to over $60,000 for more senior technical support specialists.

CHAPTER SIX

Working as a Webmaster

You can compare webmasters to ringmasters at circuses, as they are in charge of everything in their arena. The ever-changing display of information and graphics that often dazzle with special effects are their responsibility. In charge of the conceptual development as well as the day-to-day operation of websites, the webmaster is who makes sure it all happens.

Millions of Web pages are competing for attention on the Internet. It is very important for companies and individuals to have distinctive and well-run sites; otherwise, they can be lost in the sheer quantity of websites available. The webmaster is the person who creates the public image for companies and individuals on the Net. Some websites incorporate the latest in graphics and multimedia technology in an effort to capture the fleeting attention of the sophisticated cybersurfer. This type of site is often used by businesses attempting to sell a product on the Internet. Other sites may be less flashy, offering efficiency in the form of clear, simple layouts and fast links. The overall design, content, ease of use, and quality of graphics determine the public perception of the company or individual the site represents. Companies are increasingly recognizing the importance of the webmaster in projecting their online presence.

Successful websites frequently are the result of efforts by a diverse group of people, often working as a team. A typical group in a large company might include a marketing director, a technical manager, a content manager, a public relations specialist, a graphic designer, and a webmaster. It is the webmaster, however, who puts it all together. What follows is a closer look at the responsibilities of five webmasters working in diverse situations.

Webmaster for a Large Corporation

Working as a consultant in the technical department at Hewlett-Packard, Jeff Meador acts as a senior technical leader. On a typical day, he spends much of his time in meetings and on the telephone, making sure the website is developing in the way the company wants. Jeff does considerable handholding because so many people at the company need to understand how the Net can best work for them. He feels that it is important to keep a high level of personal contact and enjoys the time that he spends educating others about the Net.

The company website needs to be updated with new information two or three times a week. Press releases, product introductions, and rebate offers are commonly added to the site. While Jeff is responsible for the technical aspects, he may require an HTML programmer and a graphic artist to assist him.

In order to implement new Web technologies, Jeff needs to see what is available. He is an avid cybersurfer who spends a great deal of time surfing around the World Wide Web just to see what is out there. He finds that some new technology might offer a flashy, high-end spectacle, but it may not add substantially to the content of a website. Jeff believes that people would rather have informative sets of pages that are easily accessible. Jeff also surfs the Net in order to keep a close eye on what Hewlett-Packard's competitors are doing.

Jeff is excited by dynamic Web publishing. He has worked on a Hewlett-Packard site using this technology. Also called interactive programming, it creates Web pages that are based on information provided by the user. No two users see the same series of pages. For example, if you wanted to find a printer ribbon, you could access a website selling computer equipment. By entering the make and model of printer that you are using, the website could then show you only the ribbons appropriate for your printer.

Two or three days a week, Jeff works at Hewlett-Packard. He has no set hours but typically works an eight-hour day. When Jeff works at home, he generally works from 8:00 A.M. to 11:30 A.M. and then takes a break to go to the gym and to have lunch. He works after lunch and again at night. Jeff says that he gets more done if he works at home, but that "if you work at home, you are always at work." He feels that independent work requires an enormous amount of self-discipline and would not recommend it for everyone. When Jeff worked at home exclusively before starting at Hewlett-Packard, he needed to make an effort to develop a life outside of his job.

Learning About Computers

Jeff got an early start with computers, first playing and then designing his own games. His father drafted him for computer help, and in the process, Jeff learned how to set up a smoothly functioning office. In college, he took two classes in computer programming. When Jeff was asked to be a teaching assistant for a class in music history, he made a multimedia presentation for each class that was so successful that he was asked to assist with a literature of fantasy class taught over the Web. This work inspired Jeff to start his own business specializing in presentation consulting and the multimedia environment on the Internet. Jeff graduated from Stanford University with a degree in American studies. About a year later, he began consulting for Hewlett-Packard while still maintaining his own business.

Jeff would like to remain self-employed and to expand his company into a full agency. He says that while it is easy to get a business started, it is also easy to fall behind, and that this career choice is more work than one might imagine. His best business assets, according to Jeff, are his abilities to remain flexible and to work with people on a personal level.

Webmaster for a Telephone Company

Rhonda Davis is a personnel manager for SBC. She holds a B.S. in math and computer science and also earned an M.B.A. One of the challenges of her job is to get SBC's Web page up and running and to make sure that it is both interesting and easy to use. Working with the Web gives her both the ability to be creative and the freedom to design new processes.

Rhonda will soon add an Internet recruiting manager to her team. This person will have the primary responsibility of sourcing from the Internet as well as posting SBC jobs on the site. Rhonda sees a need for future Internet workers in the areas of marketing, sales, technical support, and teaching.

Webmaster for a Construction Company

Doug LeBlanc works as an information technology consultant for Granite Construction Company. Doug was responsible for the initial corporate website and oversees the design, management, and maintenance of the website for the heavy construction division. Doug's background includes a B.S. in engineering with a minor in math. Initially self-taught in computer programming, Doug has acquired certification in graphic design, expert systems/artificial intelligence/virtual reality, and CAD(31) design. He also has attended seminars in Internet/network design and operation. Additionally, Doug holds a fine arts certificate and has studied watercolor painting, which has been a bonus in boosting his webmaster design skills. Doug finds it challenging to maintain an efficient operating status for a diverse population of Internet and intranet users. It is also difficult to coordinate the division network operation with the corporate mainframe operation.

Doug least enjoys having to be cool when dealing with multiple requests that have emergency status to each user. He likes best feeling like a "crafty wizard" when defeating a computer glitch.

Webmaster for a Publisher

Michael McCulley is a webmaster within the Mar-Com group for Knight-Ridder Information. Michael works on the Web server, on the website, and with design and layout requirements. It is his job to edit, update, change, design, and prepare HTML and code pages for the website. He is also involved with marketing and promoting new products, services, and publications. He works with product managers, sales staff, and technical staff and spends about three hours every day on the Internet.

Michael holds a bachelor's degree in English and a master's in library science. He became involved with the Internet while he was working as a librarian at the University of California, San Diego. Michael says that keeping up with the ever-changing Internet landscape is critical for webmasters. There are always new options to be developed, which is high pressure but fun in a challenging way. To keep abreast of changes in technology, he reads E-mail, participates in mailing lists, and uses the Web daily. He says it is a great place for a librarian to work.

Michael lists these skills as a valuable mix for anyone interested in an Internet career: editorial skills, business savvy, technical skills, and Web knowledge.

Independent Webmaster

Ron Stephens runs his own business working as a webmaster. Although some of his clients are commercial businesses, the majority of them are artists interested in finding wider audiences for their work. Ron has a bachelor's degree in electrical engineering and has worked as a programmer at IBM and at Sage Instruments. While he liked programming, he wanted to work with something visual and to use some of the new tools out there. He volunteered to build a website for three local artists. His site, wwww.aptosartshoppe.com, now showcases the works of twenty-two artists. He has since built individual websites for several of the artists for fees. By volunteering at the beginning, he ended up starting a new business.

Ron enjoys working with people and pulling together a wide range of ideas to make them function as a whole. He finds he needs a lot of interface with the client. Artists, in particular, have definite ideas about the way colors, text, and images are used, and they sometimes want something changed midstream when all the pages have been set up. He then needs to go through the website page by page to make the changes. He finds it really satisfying when the page finally goes up on the Web, and he can see it for the first time. The most annoying part of his job is software that doesn't function the way it should, and he must go in and manually correct the HTML code. Before posting websites, Ron submits his pages to an HTML validator that runs an analysis and indicates what is wrong. Two websites that provide HTML validation are http://validator.w3.org and http://devedge.netscape.com.

While Ron uses FrontPage for much of his work, he stresses the need to have a solid knowledge of HTML code in order to fix problems. Other Web page authoring tools are Adobe GoLive, Macromedia Dreamweaver Mx, and Macromedia Homesite. Ron feels it is necessary to have working knowledge of Perl, JavaScripts, C++, and XML. It is also helpful to be familiar with MySQL, Active Server Page (ASP), Personal Home Page (PHP), and Cascading Style Sheets (CSS). Ron notes that you can download a free Web authoring tool called HTML_Kit from www.chami.com.

What It Takes to Be a Webmaster

If you are planning a career as a webmaster, you will find that many jobs require specific technical skills. Additionally, almost all companies stress good communication skills and the ability to work well with people, as a webmaster most often works as part of a team. While a college degree is required in many large companies, higher education is not a requirement for success in the industry as a whole. Becoming certified will aid you in getting a job or in attracting clients. Furthermore, holding certifications for the software and equipment you will be using is important.

Professional Associations

Belonging to professional organizations is often a first step toward establishing yourself in any industry, and the Internet is no exception. Two prominent organizations to consider are the Association of Web Professionals (AWP) and the Association of Internet Professionals (AIP).

The Association of Web Professionals

The Association of Web Professionals is a not-for-profit, vendor-neutral certification organization, one of several that offers certification of webmasters. The association offers certifications for Web technician, Web designer, and Web manager. The following is a brief description of the organization's qualifications for these certifications. For a complete list of required skills, see the association's website at www.jupitersystemsinc.com/awp.htm.

Certified Web Technician. A Web technician is qualified to build and maintain a Web presence. Technicians are responsible for administration, security, and ongoing support. They must be up-to-date on current network technologies and be able to set up and maintain server hardware and software, respond to E-mail problems, and perform disaster recovery.

Certified Web Designer. A Web designer is responsible for designing Web pages that are usable and reflect relevant cultural factors. The designer may work for an organization or be self-employed. To be successful, designers must stay on top of emerging trends and technologies.

The designer creates site architecture, selects and uses appropriate media, and conducts beta testing on the site. The designer must select and prepare information for inclusion and is responsible for making the site entertaining enough to generate repeat visits. designer be able to work well within a team.

Certified Web Manager. A Web manager is responsible for coordinating the planning, implementation, and maintenance of a website. The manager should be qualified in general business practices and in verbal and written communication and have good people management skills. He or she must be skilled in relevant technologies and is responsible for website security, performance, and productivity. A manager is responsible for hiring, training, and supervising the employees on the Web team.

The Association of Internet Professionals

The Webmaster Guild was founded in 1995 to educate, promote, and unify the webmaster community. It provided an active forum for Web professionals to share information within and across all Web disciplines until 1997, when it merged with the Association of Internet Professionals. AIP now has more than 250,000 individual members and over 250 corporate and educational institution members. It maintains the AIP Certification Accreditation Council, which examines the curricula and tests of educational institutions and training companies, and maintains a list of those that meet its standards. Visit the website at www.association.org to learn more about the organization and certification programs.

The Pay Scale for Webmasters

Pay levels for webmaster positions vary widely and depend on the size of the company offering the position as well as on the skill levels and responsibilities required. The average salary for an experienced webmaster is close to $70,000 per year. Entry-level webmasters earn about $35,000 per year, while a few top-level webmasters earn more than $100,000 annually.

CHAPTER SEVEN

Finance, Entertainment, and Other Net Service Careers

Everyone used to sit down at home and play games with family members, friends, and neighbors. Now, cybersurfers are going online to enjoy games with people all around the world. Looking for a job used to involve searching the want ads in the local newspaper. Today, it often means going online to see what jobs are available in your community. Are you curious about your bank balance? Your bank probably offers online banking services. Would you like to buy a plane ticket, rent a car, or make a hotel reservation? You can do it on the Internet. You can also download music, reserve movie tickets, get weather reports, and apply to college without leaving your computer.

Most bricks-and-mortar services are now available online. Plus, the number of unique services found only on the Net is expanding in many imaginative ways. You can sit at your computer and look at the surf pounding a nearby beach to decide if you want to go surfing. And if you are a businessperson, there are all kinds of services linking you to other businesses. Here are just a few examples of the thousands of services you can now access on the Net:

- beauty tips
- birthday reminders

- book reviews
- census information
- credit reports
- horoscopes
- hotel reservations
- insurance quotes
- investment advice
- legal advice
- maps
- medical advice
- movie reviews
- parenting tips
- passport applications
- sight-seeing information
- sports news and scores
- tax forms
- ticket sales
- traffic reports
- travel reservations
- weather reports

Employment Opportunities

A wide range of jobs exists in the service arena on the Net. Websites need to be built, maintained, and updated, which means jobs for programmers, webmasters, Web designers, HTML coders, technical assistants, and database architects, to name just a few. You don't have to be a technical whiz, however, to work closely with the Internet. Customer service representatives, trainers, librarians, researchers, editors, writers, and human relations and public relations workers spend much of their workdays on the Net. This chapter introduces you to just a few of the areas where you can now find jobs. Surf the Net frequently, and you will find many more innovative services that you might like to provide in an Internet-related career.

Online Financial Services

No longer do people have to visit a bank or brokerage firm; now they can turn their homes into branch banks and buy stocks and bonds using the Internet. The number of cybersurfers availing themselves of these services is rapidly increasing as they discover how much easier online financial services can make their lives. Many Internet researchers believe that financial services will become one of the most popular services offered on the Internet.

Online Banking

A new breed of banks is rapidly emerging. It began slowly back in the mid-1990s with Internet-only banks and some bricks-and-mortar banks offering online services. Basic services deal with managing checking and savings accounts. Additional services frequently include bill paying, online loan applications, and brokerage account access. In the future, as many as three-fourths of all bank customers are expected to do some of their banking online. Internet-only banks offer the advantage of low fees and great interest rates, while traditional banks offer the conveniences of online banking as well as personal contact with local bankers. Both are now adding services to draw new customers as well as making existing services more convenient, increasing job opportunities for cybersurfers.

Wells Fargo Bank. More than one hundred years ago, Wells Fargo stagecoaches traveled across the American West delivering mail and cash. Today the bank is one of the leaders in offering online banking service through the Internet. Consumers can download up-to-date information on balances and transactions for their accounts, pay bills, and transfer money between their Wells Fargo accounts. They can even develop reports and graphs showing where their money is going. Furthermore, they can have free access to some brokerage accounts and to non–Wells Fargo accounts. Plus, there are special online services for businesses, such as being able to process and settle online transactions in British pound and euro currencies. Wells Fargo first offered online banking in 1989 and Internet services in 1995. In 2001, E-mail photocopies and statements became available to customers.

Wells Fargo has several hundred employees supporting its online business. There are professionals who handle marketing, systems development, channel management, and operational management as well as employees who are responsible for customer service for the online business. Cybersurfers can visit at www.wellsfargo.com to view employment opportunities in the Internet Services division for such positions as product manager, senior applications programmer/analyst, website manager, technical support supervisor, marketing manager, and many others.

The following ad gives you an idea of what it's like to work in a job in online banking.

COMPUTER OPERATIONS ANALYST 3

Job Description: Manage multiplatform operations, scheduling, and/or data storage: monitoring, analyzing, and resolving complex production, application, and system problems to ensure data center service commitments are met. Analyze workflows and procedures and make recommendations for reruns and processing procedure improvements. Audit and maintain processing procedures/documentation within the data center for application processing and backup/contingency and resolve customer problems by initiating, resolving, and closing problem records. Provide leadership, training, and/or guidance to lower-level computer operation analysts. *Qualifications:* Bachelor's degree and three years' experience.

Online Trading and Investing

Changes are brewing in the financial market. Ever since investors became cybersurfers, they went online at thousands of websites to get information and advice that once was only available from a broker or to professional investors. On the Net, investors were able to get market quotes, analyses, and predictions and to participate in discussion forums. Late in 1995, cybersurfers had the additional opportunity to buy and sell stocks, securities, and mutual funds. Acceptance of online trading and investing was so rapid that by the end of 1996 there were an estimated 1.5 million online brokerage accounts, and this figure grew close to an astonishing 20 million accounts in the United States by 2001. The current trend is for online trading firms to offer more financial services as well as more trading advice and information.

Job Opportunities. As online brokerage soared, so did the number of jobs in this field. However, with the downturn of the economy in the early 2000s, layoffs and hiring freezes became common as earnings tumbled. You can expect this pattern to continue in the future, with more jobs in good economic times. To see what types of jobs are available for cybersurfers at online brokerage firms, explore employment opportunities at these major players:

Charles Schwab	www.schwab.com
E∗Trade	www.etrade.com
TD Waterhouse	www.waterhouse.com
Fidelity Investments	www.fidelity.com
Ameritrade, Inc.	www.ameritrade.com

E∗Trade. E∗Trade is considered the pioneer of online brokerage firms. The first online trade using the company's technology was placed back in 1983. In 1992, E∗Trade began offering online investing services through America Online and CompuServe. The advent of the Internet brought www.etrade.com online. E∗Trade offers online trading; a range of portfolio management tools; and access to company research, market analysis, news, and other information services anytime, anywhere, and with any device twenty-four hours a day, seven days a week. Customers can also access their accounts via a network of more than eleven thousand E*Trade ATMs and kiosks. Click on "About Us" and then "Jobs" to see employment opportunities, including the possibility of being an intern. You might see a job like the one in the following ad.

NETWORK ENGINEER

Department: Product Development/IT

Job Description: Provide engineering and troubleshooting support for network infrastructure. Provide operational support for international and domestic network consisting of Internet commerce and business LAN connectivity. Compile statistics and reports on the network performance and utilization of all network circuits and related equipment. Maintain network troubleshooting equipment and tools. *Qualifications:* B.A. or B.S. preferred. Two to five years' experience in networking. Knowledge of WAN, ISPs, Cisco routers, Catalyst 5000s, BGP, ATM, and network management technologies. Ability to analyze information from network management tools and draw conclusions about network performance and trends. Implementation and problem resolution of high-speed TCP/IP (especially EIGRP/BGP) connections. Working knowledge of DNS, http, https, and UNIX and NT. Skilled in using HPOpenview, Network General Sniffer, NetMatrix, and Cisco Works. Team player. Good written and verbal communications skills. Good interpersonal skills.

Online Entertainment Services

Cybersurfers who are movie or television addicts, sports buffs, or online game players should look into the job opportunities that are appearing at all the companies now bringing entertainment to the Internet.

Jobs at Entertainment Websites

Radio and television stations have staked out territory on the World Wide Web to provide news, weather, stock updates, and entertainment news as well as the opportunity to listen to programs online. Movie studios have come aboard the Net to publicize their films and stars. Companies are streaming movies to your computer, turning the monitor into a TV screen. Plus, all your favorite TV shows are likely to have websites to let you know more about present and past episodes and series stars and even to let you buy related merchandise. In fact, everything that you want to know about a film or TV show is probably on some website.

If you are a cybersurfer who is fascinated by entertainment news and celebrity gossip, a job at an entertainment website may be right for you. There are opportunities in writing, editing, designing, engineering, and Web production positions. Go online to such sites as E! Online (www.eonline.com) and Hollywood.com (www.hollywood.com) to investigate jobs in this arena.

Jobs at Sports Websites

The most popular entertainment websites are those catering to the millions of sports fans eager to receive the latest news about their favorite teams and sports stars.

You will find thousands of sports-related sites operated by professional leagues, sports magazines, major media, small companies, and individuals. There are sites for every sport, from baseball to croquet to water polo. All of these sites are loaded with statistics, commentary, player information, and live chat facilities. Sports fans can also access real-time scores and highlights as well as participate in fantasy games.

ESPN.com. One of the most popular spots on the Internet, ESPN.com (www.espn.com) averages millions of hits every day. It offers sports news, stats, and scores that are constantly being updated. It provides exclusive analysis from ESPN's experts, contests, online chat, and live audio game broadcasts. At ESPN.com, it is possible to combine a love of sports with skills and interest in technology and the Internet. For job information, go to "Jobs" on the ESPN.com website, where you might see a listing like the one in the following ad.

ASSOCIATE PHOTO EDITOR

Job Description: Research, crop, compress, color correct, and post photos for EIG websites as directed by the managing photo editor.

Qualifications: The ideal candidate will have proven experience locating appropriate photos using online wire services and must know the latest compression techniques for efficient downloading of Web images. The candidate will be expected to crop and compress photos using Photoshop and Debabelizer. The ideal candidate will have a four-year degree in art production or graphic design. Must have good organizational and communication skills, be highly motivated, and function independently. Will be expected to work non-traditional hours, including weekends and holidays. A knowledge of sports is required.

Public Relations Assistant at a Sports Website. Jobs that let cybersurfers work on the Net all day are not always obvious. One of these jobs is the entry-level position of public relations assistant. In this job, you would handle press releases, field media calls, set up speeches for executives, and work on public relations strategies with outside firms. Approximately 75 percent of your workday could be spent on the Net because you have to know what is out there, from company site content to articles about your company to online publications. You might also have to update the corporate site, requiring some knowledge of HTML.

A Unique Online Service—Surf Information. The successful companies providing services on the Internet are those that have found a niche that draws cybersurfers. This service niche can draw a large group, such as investors, sports fans, or travelers. Or it can attract a smaller group, such as serious surfers—ocean surfers, that is. Understanding surfers' needs for surf information and forecasts led Surfline to put comprehensive surf information on the Internet at www.surfline.com in 1995. If you take a quick tour of the site, you will note that it includes all the information you need to make plans for your next surfing session, including conditions, forecasts, live cams, weather maps, tide charts, and the like. Plus, you can shop at a surfing store, make travel arrangements, visit the video vault, and communicate with fellow surfers and surfing experts.

Surfline was started in 1985 by Sean Collins and Jerry Arnold, two ardent surfers, to provide recorded surf information on the phone. They employed a network of one hundred part-time surf watchers who checked the surf around the world two or three times a day and then called an area coordinator, who put the information into a script for the 900-number phone service. In 1996, one year after expanding beyond their traditional phone service and launching a website, the company debuted the world's first surfcam—featuring live, full-color images of the surf at Huntington Pier. The number of visitors to the website skyrocketed when surfers all over the world discovered that they could see live images of California beaches. And the numbers continue to grow with more than one million unique visitors now surfing the site each month. Today, there are more than three thousand sites that link directly to Surfline.com.

The original website was developed by an outside company; however, the West Coast coordinators, along with a coordinator on the East Coast, did the updates. With success, the number of employees at the company has grown to include a tech team of four employees who completely rebuilt the Surfline.com website, a surf reporting/forecasting team, a meteorologist, a product manager, an environmental editor, an HTML producer, and a sales and marketing staff. Sean serves as president, chief weather editor, and wave forecaster. In 1999, this successful Internet pioneer was named one of the "25 Most Influential Surfers of the Century." He also was named the 2002 "Eighth Most Powerful Person in Surfing" by *Surfer Magazine*. Surfline.com also received a "Webby" for being the best sporting online website in 2001.

Jobs at Online Game Websites

The millions of game players who have become accustomed to playing video games now have the opportunity to play single- and multiplayer games online. And besides playing games, they can enter contests and gaming competitions, chat with other players, keep track of stats in different games, find news about games and game strategies, download the latest game demos, and buy game-associated products. To get an idea of all the services available online that cater to the interests of gaming enthusiasts, visit the GameSpy Arcade at www.gamespyarcade.com or IGN Entertainment at www.ign.com. And remember that each of these services represents possible jobs for cybersurfers like you. There is a good employment outlook, too. Analysts expect phenomenal growth in online gaming because of the tremendous consumer demand and technological advancements fueling that growth.

Creating Games. The creation of games is a team effort that involves designers, programmers, graphic artists, animators, musicians, sound technicians, directors, producers, play testers, and even actors. Some of these jobs are done in-house, while others are done by freelancers. At companies that create games, there are also jobs for those who work on the business side.

Editorial Director of an Online Gaming Company. While in college majoring in cognitive science and computer science, Chris Lombardi got a headstart on his future by working part-time as an editorial assistant at *Computer Gaming World* (*CGW*) magazine, where he was a receptionist, subscription clerk, mailroom boy, and gofer. After graduation, he became an online projects manager assigned to bring the *CGW* materials to the Prodigy online service. Sadly, just as the project was going to launch, Prodigy fired a large portion of its staff, including most of the game staff, and the games area of Prodigy was never fully implemented. This was Chris's first experience of the speed with which things can change in the online world. After the Prodigy project, he became an associate editor and then eighteen months later the editor, which made him responsible for the overall "look and feel" of the magazine.

Chris left the magazine world to become the editorial director at a company that had paying subscribers for their action, strategy, simulation, and role-playing PC games. In this job, he had three major responsibilities:

1. **Create editorial materials related to games on the company's service.** His team of six editors wrote strategy and tips articles, news about games and events on the website, and support materials, such as "Help" and "ReadMe" files.
2. **Create and administer events on the game service.** His staff developed ideas for game tournaments and contests and then worked with the marketing group to make these events happen.
3. **Evaluate new games for the company.** His team acted as the "gaming experts" for the company. Before a new game was brought on the game site, the team made sure it was a quality product and appropriate for online gaming.

In order to handle his responsibilities, Chris worked between fifty-five and sixty-five hours a week. A lot of his time was spent on the Net. Throughout the day, he went online to do research, put up new editorial materials, get information from the company's intranet, and see how things were going on the site. He had continual contact with the artists and designers, the marketing team, the people who developed relationships with game companies and brought new games to the company, and various members of the technology staff, including programmers, HTML writers, and database managers.

Online Employment Services

Job hunting using the Internet has really taken off and changed how professional, managerial, and technical people look for work. It is a rare college student who has not visited an Internet job board in his or her search for a job after graduation, during the school year, or during summer vacation. The Net is also changing the way unskilled workers find jobs, as government employment agencies in every state now have huge lists of job openings online for positions from fast-food workers to assembly-line workers. Furthermore, a national job market is being created as access to the Internet is letting job seekers find jobs in every state. In fact, searching for a job online has become an accepted practice, with millions of job seekers visiting online job sites each month.

Opportunities for jobs at an Internet career site can be found at the largest job boards: Monster (www.monster.com), HotJobs (www.hotjobs.com), and Career Boards (www.careerboards.com), as well as much smaller niche job sites. Plus, many big companies now have their own Internet job boards, increasing the range of job possibilities for cybersurfers.

JOBTRAK—Online Job Listing Service

When Ken Ramberg graduated from college in 1987, he saw first-hand the inefficient way employers had to post job listings separately to different universities. Along with two partners, he started JOBTRAK in 1988 as a central data processing center that transmitted job listings to colleges via modem for storage on each university's local PC database. With the advent of the Internet,

JOBTRAK developed a Gopher system to access the database and then went aboard the World Wide Web when it became available. Soon, most major university career centers teamed up with JOB-TRAK to process job listings and make them available to their job seekers both via the Web and in hard copy. By 1996 more than 500,000 job openings were posted on the service, and students and young alumni could also work on their resumes, find out how to negotiate a salary, or prepare for an interview. JOBTRAK created partnerships with college placement centers, allowing employers to target their job listings to any or all of the member campuses throughout the country. By 1997, more than 250,000 employers had used JOBTRAK, paying a small fee per campus per listing.

From JOBTRAK to MonsterTRAK. In 2001, JOBTRAK joined with Monster.com, the leading global online careers website, to launch MonsterTRAK (www.monstertrak.com) with Ken Ramberg as president of the new venture. The goal was the same as JOBTRAK's—to connect students with employers who were actively seeking their skills and to give employers a highly effective recruiting tool. The new company added career center partners at colleges faster than ever and was soon handling approximately 1.5 million visits a month. There were also free job postings for the elderly and disabled, and campus volunteer centers could post volunteer opportunities for free on MonsterTRAK. Today, MonsterTRAK is the largest website for students and recent graduates to find jobs targeted to specific colleges or universities.

The Jobs Picture at MonsterTRAK. When JOBTRAK started, the company had four employees. One was a programmer and the rest were out trying to get business. By 1997, there were more than eighty-five employees, which illustrates how rapidly the company grew. Besides top management and office and human resources managers, JOBTRAK had five full-time programmers—all in their twenties. Two were originally hired as interns. The programmers integrated the database with the Net, which required them to keep abreast of the latest technological changes. There were three trainers who taught the customer service employees to do basic troubleshooting, which involved answering questions about the website and helping students and alumni navigate the Net and create resumes. The customer service employees, who needed to have a broad knowledge of the Internet, were also taught how to take phone listings and enter them into the database. The other two employees worked in college relations and visited college career centers demonstrating JOBTRAK and trying to bring aboard new colleges. Today, the number of employees has grown immensely. For example, the job development force at Monster-TRAK is now several hundred people strong.

Online Information Services

When professionals need to know something and to know it right away, they go online to use information services that can access millions of documents not available through Web search engines. The largest services include LEXISNexis (www.lexisnexis.com), Dialog (www.dialog.com), and Factiva (www.factiva.com). Their information is broad, deep, and growing constantly. For example, LEXISNexis has more than a billion documents online in thousands of databases and adds millions of documents each week. There are also smaller information services that specialize in narrow subject areas. All offer a wide range of employment opportunities to match the skills and interests of cybersurfers, whether they are technical gurus who want to work with databases, systems support, or software development, or others who want to be closely involved with the Internet as customer service representatives, marketing and sales team members, or researchers.

Most information services list career opportunities on their Web pages. Study the educational qualifications carefully because they often require advanced college degrees or considerable technological skills. For example, a customer support position might require you to be a lawyer, financial specialist, librarian, or computer specialist as well as have an excellent knowledge of Word, Excel, and Outlook, plus good oral and written communication skills. And a technology position in telecom development/support could require knowledge of ATM, Ethernet, FDDI, LAN, WAN, X-25, TCP/IP, and electronic commerce.

Online Car Buying Services

Buying a car used to be a hassle, with customers having to search for the vehicle they want and then engage in a prolonged haggle to get the best price. Now it is possible to find and even purchase the perfect car online. Because two out of three car buyers are already surfing the Web before even visiting a dealership and the number of online purchases of vehicles is steadily growing, the outlook for a career in this area is excellent. Car manufacturers have websites with detailed information about their vehicles that are becoming more popular. However, consumers seem to prefer going to independent sites such as www.consumerreports.org, www.edmunds .com, and www.kbb.com to compare the prices and values of both new and used cars. The company, however, that is the leader in visits for both online research and buying services is Autobytel, Inc. (www.autobytel.com), which owns and operates four websites. Aubobytel.com offers consumer resources for vehicle research, purchasing, ownership, safety, and maintenance, as well as dealer training, support, and technology. Autoweb.com has multibrand, third-party automotive E-commerce sites that appeal to research-driven buyers. CarSmart.com is known for its authoritative vehicle data, and Autosite.com serves as a comprehensive research resource for entry-level buyers looking to begin the online purchasing process.

CarSmart—from Start-Up to Major Player

CarSmart went online at www.carsmart.com in the third quarter of 1996 to assist consumers in locating, pricing, purchasing, and leasing new or used vehicles. By January of 1997, the website was receiving more than twenty thousand requests a day from consumers wanting to find nearby dealers who had specific vehicles. In order to handle this business, CarSmart had fifteen full-time employees and was looking for more. The employees included a head programmer and four support programmers, an advertising analyst, six salespeople to sign up more deals, four dealer assistant coordinators, and three data-entry people. The president, who was one of the founders of CarSmart, coordinated the entire process.

In 1999, CarSmart was acquired by Autobytel.com. There's been a slow integration until all the CarSmart employees became employees of one company, Autobytel Inc. Recent college graduates will find the most job opportunities at Autobytel.com in the tech and sales sides of the company. Because this is a large company, you'll also be able to find jobs in administration. And to your delight, most jobs involve some online surfing.

Online Auctions and Giant eBay

If you have a cameo necklace from your grandmother or a watch fob from your great-uncle and no desire ever to wear either one, you may be able to auction each valuable piece of jewelry online. While there are many sites auctioning items from soda pop cans to diamond rings, the absolute giant in this growing field is eBay (www.ebay.com).

The company was founded in 1995 with the mission of helping practically anyone trade practically anything on Earth. It has turned into the most popular shopping site on the Internet and has more than forty-nine million registered users. On any given day, there are millions of items listed on eBay across thousands of categories. People go to the site to buy and sell. In addition, the site offers other features, such as eBay Stores, which allow sellers to create customized shopping destinations to merchandise their items on eBay, and Buy It Now, which lets buyers buy an item at a specified price without having to wait for the end of an auction.

Because eBay has become such a large company, it has listings for a wide variety of jobs on its website, including jobs for content management systems engineers, software engineers, administrative assistants, and business and financial analysts.

More Online Services

As more and more people go online, new services are constantly emerging to enhance their use of the Internet. If there is something that you want to buy online at the very best price, there are services such as NexTag (www.nextag.com), which does comparison shopping for you. Paying bills by check is rapidly disappearing as online companies handle this monthly task for you.

When companies want to make conference calls to a large number of clients, an Internet service such as Connect-us (www.callconnect-us.com) makes it easy. You can also have content delivered directly from the Internet to your computer. Many of the companies that deliver services started small and have turned into giants, and new ones are constantly being created by cybersurfers like you who are fascinated by the Internet.

Interpage Network Services— Telecommunications-Based Services

Because the Internet is such a new and dynamic organism, creative young people can have an idea, implement it, and discover that they have developed a successful company. While taking a car trip one day, Doug Reuben wondered what E-mail had arrived on his computer at home. He had a pager with him that provided information about phone calls. Doug soon came up with the idea of putting E-mail messages on pagers and fax machines, and Interpage Network Services (www.interpage.net) was born. A programmer friend, Doug Fields, became his partner and together they developed the necessary software to link E-mail with pagers and fax machines. Doug Fields did part of the coding, and Doug Reuben debugged and tested and refined the code.

Doug Reuben did administrative work and responded to news-group postings on technical communications issues relevant to the new company. He also set up links to many websites. The cost for starting the company was approximately $15,000. At first, Doug and his partner gave away the new service to get customers. Once the business became established, the company saw other niches and added more services for Internet users, including an online shopping service, a site and server monitoring service, a fax mailbox, and the delivery of news, weather, stock, or personal reminders from the Web to pagers and fax machines. All of the day-to-day work of Interpage was automatic, except getting and keeping customers.

In 1997, this fledgling company had eight employees. Besides the owners, there were two customer service representatives, two systems supervisors, a billing clerk, and a staff member to handle large accounts. At that time, Doug saw the company developing into a complete communications service to businesses with all of Interpage's services oriented toward the continued integration of the Internet with traditional communications media. This has happened.

Today, Interpage is an enhanced Internet gateway service that sends, receives, and integrates E-mail and Web-based messages and content to customers from their pagers, fax machines, regular and international cell phones, and more. For example, a deli restaurant that has customers E-mail in orders may not want to be constantly checking online for orders. Interpage receives the restaurant's E-mail orders and automatically faxes them to the restaurant so they can easily be filled. There are also services that let customers have weather, stock, news, and other information sent to their pagers, fax machines, or E-mail accounts at any time of day, whenever they want it, as well as many other services that are described on the Interpage website.

As the number of businesses using Interpage's services has steadily increased, the number of full- and part-time employees has grown to eighteen. There is now a technical staff that writes code and sees that everything is working, two salespeople, and more customer service representatives. Doug is the overall administrator. His main focus is on strategic planning and especially on building sufficient redundancy into the company so that its services will never be down.

Electronic Payments

A very hot growth area on the Net is the presenting and paying of bills online. Consumers and businesses are simply abandoning checks for electronic payments. And experts expect paying online to become the rule, not the exception, in the near future. According to a Federal Reserve System survey, there has been a 25 percent drop in check usage since 1979. This move to paperless bill paying has increased job opportunities for cybersurfers at banks and online bill payment service providers. There is a special need for programmers to implement this technology and to integrate it with existing customer services.

PayPal—Sending and Receiving Payments Online. Any consumer or business with an E-mail address can send and receive payments online by using PayPal (www.paypal.com). The firm, owned by eBay, is the leading payment network for online auction websites and is also used at many E-commerce sites for the sale of goods. Doctors, lawyers, and contractors have increasingly begun to receive payments online through PayPal. The online payments revolution has made it possible for cybersurfers to find careers at the company in these areas:

- business development
- credit/risk management
- customer service operations
- engineering/programming
- finance
- information systems
- legal

- marketing
- product management
- Web content/design

College Admissions Services

For students thinking about college, looking for the right college, registering for admissions tests, practicing for admissions tests, finding scholarships or financial aid, or applying for admission, the process can now be done almost totally online. Two websites that offer so many of these services are the Princeton Review at www.princetonreview.com and the College Board at www .collegeboard.com. Diverse career opportunities are offered on both websites.

Preparing for a Job Providing Internet Services

The first step in getting a job with a company that provides Internet services is to become "Netwise," which should be an enjoyable task for cybersurfers and other online types. No matter what your job, you need to be able to navigate around the Internet and handle E-mail. The second step is to surf through the employment and jobs pages of companies that interest you to see exactly what qualifications they are seeking. While college is a prerequisite for most positions, many people have gained the required technical expertise through their own cybersurfing and computer experiences. A man who was formerly the janitor at a small company now maintains another company's extensive Web setup because he knew enough HTML to say, "Yes, I can do that," when he was asked for help. When you look at job ads, notice that, in addition to technical skills, most employers are looking for employees who have good oral and written communications skills and organizational skills.

Here is some solid advice for cybersurfers who would like to quickly climb the Internet corporate ladder: *Breadth! Breadth! Breadth!* Get as much experience in as many areas as possible—technology, writing, project management, and art. Specialization in one field or another might get you a good job, but it's the generalists who have a broad base of knowledge and can bring it to bear on new problems who will get to do the most interesting work. The best way to acquire this knowledge is to learn as you earn. Get a low-level job in an interesting company and take every opportunity you can to learn. Keep your eyes open, talk to your manager, volunteer for any task that will extend your experience. Always think about your job, no matter what it is, in terms of the big picture and the broader company goals. At many online companies, receptionists can be promoted into new jobs and different areas of the company—marketing, customer support, product development—because they are smart, eager, hardworking people.

CHAPTER EIGHT

E-Commerce Careers

O nline shopping continues to gain in popularity as cyber-surfers increasingly appreciate its convenience and money-saving opportunities. In fact, E-commerce has been one of the healthy survivors of the recent dot-com disasters. Although a number of E-commerce businesses have shut down their websites, new ones continue to emerge as more and more online users are turning into online shoppers. And they are discovering a wide array of products—even items not readily available in bricks-and-mortar stores, such as odd-sized shoes, robots, and supplies for a fondue party.

If you are considering a career in E-commerce, it's important to understand that shopping on the Internet is just in its infancy—it's a business that only really started in the mid-1990s. It was as recent as 1995 that Jeff Bezos started Amazon.com to sell books on the Web. Fewer than half of the online users in the United States today are actually making online purchases. However, the potential for far more customers is enormous as more and more people become acquainted with buying online. Market research firms don't agree on how much merchandise is now being sold, but all agree that sales will skyrocket in the years ahead.

Today, E-commerce presents you with the opportunity to be an entrepreneur and start your own company. Thousands have successfully taken this route. You also have the opportunity to work for both large and small online retailers as well as established bricks-and-mortar retailers, such as Macy's and Sears, which also sell products online.

Becoming an Internet Entrepreneur

While the opportunities are decidedly there for individuals to own successful Internet businesses, there are several reality checks for future Net entrepreneurs. Sales on the Internet are not booming yet. There are still more browsers than shoppers in most online stores. Only a very few companies are making a profit in cyberspace. It is not easy to establish a successful online business—knowledge, dedication, and hard work are the key ingredients.

Step One: Learning About the Internet

If you are thinking of becoming an entrepreneur and selling a product on the Internet or would like to work for a company that does, you must have some knowledge of how the Net works. This does not mean that you must become a technical guru; however, you should be at home navigating the Net, as most cybersurfers are. If you aren't, there are books such as *The Internet for Dummies* by John R. Levine that give Internet newcomers the basic information they need to get started. Or visit www.learnthenet.com to master the basics, learn how to surf the Net, and handle E-mail from tutorials and articles. Also, it is possible to take classes or even hire a private tutor to help you discover how to be a cybersurfer. Many public libraries have docent programs to teach individuals how to use the Net. Training others to use the Internet is discussed as a career option in Chapter 9.

If you are a technical whiz, it will be easy for you to get your business online. If you aren't, there are loads of experts ready to help you. Before consulting one, read about the services you will need in such books as *Starting an Online Business for Dummies* by Greg Holden, *Marketing on the Internet* by Jill H. Ellsworth and Matthew V. Ellsworth, or *The Complete E-Commerce Book: Design, Build, and Maintain a Successful Web-Based Business* by Janice Reynolds and Roya Mofazali. Or you can go aboard the Internet and ask your questions in a chat room or find more information in the previously mentioned learnthenet.com website.

Step Two: Assessing the Competition

You don't have to be a seasoned businessperson to become an entrepreneur on the Net. You could be a college student or even a high school student—many have started their own businesses. According to marketing experts, one of the biggest secrets to making money on the Net is to offer something that is unique. Instead of just selling records, Tower Records (www.towerrecords.com) offers customers free shipping for purchases over a certain amount, as well as helpful lists of records in a great number of categories to make the selection process easier. In addition to selling their products on the Net, many companies, especially flower and gift stores, are also offering to send you E-mail reminders of special events such as birthdays and anniversaries.

The best way for you to get an idea of all the products being sold on the Internet and discover what your own product niche might be is to visit an online shopping mall, also known as a cybermall. When you get to a cybermall, browse through the directory and you'll quickly discover the immense variety of items being sold in such categories as appliances, arts, automotive, clothing, electronics, fashion and beauty, food and drink, home improvement, and sporting goods. Some large general malls you might visit include the Internet Mall at www.internetmall.com, Galaxy Mall at www.galaxymall.com, and 21st Century Plaza at www.21stcenturyplaza.com.

At present, the highest sales are enjoyed by companies selling products in these categories: software, books, music, videos, airline tickets, car reservations, hotel reservations, computer hardware, consumer electronics, office supplies, apparel, footwear, jewelry, and home decorations. Look at the stores in these areas carefully. Caution: If your product will not sell in a real-world store or a catalog, it won't sell online either. You must choose a product that will appeal to your potential online customers. Typically, they are between eighteen and forty-nine, well educated, and well off. They are also likely to be employed in educational, computer-related, or professional or management occupations.

More than half of your customers will be male; however, the number of female online shoppers is steadily growing.

Step Three: Acquiring Internet Marketing Savvy

Prospective entrepreneurs must understand that there is a steep learning curve to becoming a marketing expert. You need to know the basics of the marketing process, from market research to making sales. Beyond this, you need to understand that the Net introduces a new note into marketing interactivity: buyers and sellers can communicate with each other any time, day or night. And sales websites must let prospective customers point and click to find ever more product information, which is personalized to meet the needs of different customers. For example, some car buyers on the Net are interested in economy and gas mileage, while safety considerations are foremost for others. It is also important that product information can be accessed in a reasonable period of time. Customers do not want to spend time waiting while fancy graphic images slowly become visible.

Another important aspect of Internet marketing is knowing how to get publicity for your company's website so that shoppers will visit and, hopefully, make purchases. Just being part of a shopping mall won't do it, as malls often have thousands of stores. Cybersurfers-turned-entrepreneurs must understand some of the tried-and-true methods involving print, radio, and TV media, as well as newer methods associated with the Net. Here are a few suggestions:

- Advertise in computer and Internet magazines.
- Publicize your site to the media (you can use E-mail to do this).
- Register yourself in as many directories as possible.
- Cross-link your site with companies that complement yours.

- Advertise on welcome screens where users log on to a service.
- Get on mailing lists.
- Visit EPage's site at http://ep.com/faq/webannounce.html to discover online how to announce your new website in great detail.

You may be able to find a newsgroup that permits advertisement or a low-key mention of products or services. Caution: Avoid "spamming," which is the inappropriate posting of advertisements. In other words, you should follow the rules of "Netiquette," the informal rules for Net behavior. This includes avoiding sending unsolicited E-mail. The books and websites mentioned earlier in this chapter give you a good idea of some of the fundamentals of marketing a product online successfully.

Step Four: Setting Up Your Internet Business

Like all businesses, setting up an Internet business is quite complicated. You need a business plan that details what you are going to do and how you will do it. Fortunately, for cybersurfers interested in starting their own businesses, there is a gold mine of information on the Internet directed at helping you do business on the Net. You can spend time on the Internet while gathering valuable start-up information at these sites:

- **Michael Learner Productions** (www.learnthenet.com) tackles the issue of making money online in its "Do E-Business" area. Solid advice on understanding copyrights, getting professional advice, designing for different audiences, finding a site on the World Wide Web for a business, maintenance and updating, and publicizing a site is featured in the "Build a Website" area.
- *Inc. Magazine* (www.inc.com) offers information from more than five thousand articles dating back to 1986, which

you can access by searching by company name, management topic, or industry. There are interactive worksheets and checklists in "Tools" to teach you more ways to be smart about business. Besides recommending sites for finding specific legal information, government agencies, and more, an E-commerce starter kit can help you find the right strategies for starting your business.

- **The National Federation of Independent Business** (www.nfibonline.com) offers free insurance guides as well as online workshops in such areas as starting a business. It has a database of educational information on owning and operating a small business. Plus, there are custom workshops and tutorials.

- **Small Business Administration** (www.sbaonline.sba.gov) has such areas of interest as starting and financing your business. It also features the addresses of local centers offering training and counseling resources as well as a business advisor section with FAQs on federal agencies.

- **Idea Café: The Small Business Channel** (www.ideacafe .com) offers a fun approach to serious business and at the same time has handy information on financing and starting and running a business for aspiring entrepreneurs. You can use the "Cyberschmooz" area to ask questions and share tips, and "Coffee Talk" presents the chance to talk with the experts. In the "Financing Sources" area, there is information on borrowing money, getting investors, and learning about other sources of money.

- **U.S. Business Advisor** (www.business.gov) exists to provide business with one-stop access to federal government information, services, and transactions. The goal is to make the relationship between business and government more productive. Here you will find forms and publications from the IRS and other tools, guides, and forms to help you solve problems and do business with the government.

- **SCORE Counselors to America's Small Business**
  (www.score.org) is an organization composed of retired
  executives dedicated to aiding in the formation, growth, and
  success of small businesses nationwide. The website offers
  business how-to articles and subscriptions to a newsletter
  giving tips, ideas, and resources to help you build your
  business. It also tells you how to find the local chapter in
  your area that can provided one-on-one personal help, as
  well as workshops and other activities.

Step Five: Creating the Home Page

The home page, or website, can be thought of as your cyberstore.
It's the online spot where you present your product or products in
text, graphics, and possibly sound and video. It isn't just one page
but as many pages as are needed to fully describe your product or
products. Customers can move from page to page using hypertext
links that allow them to find the information they want.

Having interesting and well-designed pages is important to
your sales success. The material on your pages has to be converted
to HTML (hypertext markup language), the programming language that must be used so Web browsers on other computers can
read your material. If you lack the expertise to convert files to
HTML or lack sufficient design experience to create attractive
pages, you may wish to hire a Web designer or consultant. Chapter 5 describes the services these individuals offer.

Finally, before placing your home page on the Net, try it out.
Make sure every element works. You don't want customers to discover that nothing happens when they click on a particular item.
Ask others associated with your business to check out your page,
looking especially for confusing instructions or information.

Step Six: Opening Your Online Business

Once your home page is created, you are ready to open your
cyberstore. Of course, you will need a computer and modem to

access the Internet unless you elect to have someone else operate your business. You are most likely to access the Net through an Internet service provider. Chapter 2 describes the many marketing and technical services that ISPs offer.

You can get your store on the Internet in several ways. Commercial online services will put you on the Net as well as maintain the hardware, software, and security for your cyberstore. This is probably the least expensive way to get into business. Another option is leasing a space in a cybermall. Besides hosting your site and providing similar services to commercial online services, these malls usually advertise the mall stores, run promotions to attract people to the mall, and may handle credit card transactions. In addition, some will help in the design of your home page. It is also possible to connect directly to the Internet, but this is a very expensive option that is best for large companies.

Learning Firsthand About Doing Business on the Internet

There is no shortage of information about doing business on the Internet in computer and Internet magazines and books and on the Internet itself. However, to help you understand what is truly involved in becoming an Internet entrepreneur, here are the stories of several individuals who are business successes on the Net. Only one of these businesspeople is an Internet guru. All, however, are savvy marketers who see the Internet playing an important role in selling products.

A Purveyor of Quality Web Resources

Thomas Boutell, a programmer by profession, can be considered a World Wide Web pioneer. Back in late 1992, when there was hardly a Web and there were no Web browsers for common personal computers, he produced the first nontechnical magazine on the World Wide Web just for fun. Then during 1993 and 1994, he enjoyed maintaining the World Wide Web List of Frequently Asked Questions (FAQs). His skill in handling FAQs built his reputation, and Thomas discovered that what he'd been doing for fun was in demand. So he decided to take control of his own time and quit his job to write a book, *CGI Programming in C and Perl*, and expand his Web efforts into a full-time endeavor. The book advance gave him the opportunity to turn his early freeware programs into more advanced commercial versions. These programs dealt with Web design and with Web server statistics. The new software was placed on the Net as shareware (downloadable software for which users are expected to pay a registration fee). Gradually, Thomas realized that he had a business as more and more money began to come in from registration of the shareware. His wife, who has also worked in the software industry, joined him in this project and took charge of the financial side of the business, which was incorporated properly in 1995 as Boutell.Com, Inc. (www.boutell.com). By 1996, the firm took off, and his company became a Net business success story.

During the Internet boom times, Thomas served as company president, his wife was the treasurer, and his sister and others managed the office, handling the day-to-day operation of the company. This included answering the phone, taking orders, serving as customer service representative, and maintaining the database of the rapidly growing business. Another employee was a half-time software developer.

With the downturn in the computer industry, Thomas downsized his company. He is now spending about half of his time programming and the rest handling the day-to-day responsibilities of the company. He is also experimenting with automating more of his company paperwork. The company headquarters is now in his home. From time to time, he answers technical support calls, which gives him a close look at what customers think of his product. Looking into the future, Thomas sees himself spending a major part of his time upgrading software to keep his customers satisfied, as well as writing another book.

Although Thomas is a skilled programmer, he hired contract graphic designers to create his Web pages. He also uses them when he needs icons and product logos. He chooses to hire this work out because he wants quality graphics and design on his pages that will download in a reasonable amount of time. His advice to fledgling entrepreneurs is to keep your "day job" until the time demands and financial success of your new business are so great that you simply must go full-time for yourself.

A Closer Look at the Net Business. Boutell.Com is in the business of selling software that primarily deals with Web log analysis (gathering statistics on the number of people visiting a website). Thomas is the major writer of this software, which is mostly purchased by Web-hosting companies and individual webmasters. From the home page, prospective customers can access a description of the company's many programs and then select those they would like to learn more about. When customers wish to look at or purchase a product, they can download it to their computers immediately. The registration fee for using the software is then sent to the company over the Net. If customers do not pay the fee and receive a certain code from the company, the software just stops working in thirty days. Eighty percent of the sales of this software are generated online. The remaining sales come from phone and mail orders.

The Company's Ideals. Dedicated to the ideas of "voluntary simplicity" and responsible environmentalism, Boutell.Com is a nearly paperless office that recycles as much as possible, reuses many materials, and obtains much of its noncritical equipment from thrift stores and yard sales. The company donates 10 percent of its net after-tax profits to nonprofit and charitable organizations. To promote its ideals most directly, Boutell.Com provides discount prices on several software programs to users in nonprofit and educational organizations.

Bears by the Sea

In 1992, Kitty Wilde and a partner launched a retail store in Pismo Beach, California, to sell collectible teddy bears. The store also sells such bear-related items as stamps, books, and jewelry, as well as a large selection of plush animals and Beanie Babies and several beanie-related accessory items and books. In 1995, Kitty brought Bears by the Sea online (www.bearsbythesea.com) to complement the retail store. The idea was to generate more income as well as to funnel people into the store.

Kitty had prior experience in starting several businesses, so she knew the importance of creating a business plan before going online. However, she had no computer experience and didn't even own a computer. A webmaster made a sample site in just twenty minutes, which truly impressed her. Then her partner, who had never set up a website before, worked with the webmaster to create the equivalent of thirty hard-copy pages while Kitty decided what should be featured on the site. This initial website cost $1,200. The only other expenses were buying a laptop computer, so she could handle the business anywhere, and securing an Internet service provider that offered unlimited local access. Within two weeks of contacting the webmaster, Bears by the Sea was online.

To draw attention to her online store, Kitty put her website address on business cards, magazine ads, handouts, and just about everywhere. She also made sure that her company was listed in the right search engines and directories. Soon people were calling and offering to pay for links to their sites, as Bears by the Sea was such a high-traffic site.

Kitty soon became computer literate, spending two to three hours a day in Net activities. Most of her time was spent answering E-mail, but she also had to process orders, answer questions from her online forum, and evaluate what items to feature on the website. Marketing was another ongoing responsibility, which involved looking at other sites and for new search engines as well as E-mailing other sites for possible links. All of her efforts paid off. Soon, 25 percent or more of her sales were from online customers, and many new customers visited her store because they saw the website. You can learn more about Bears by the Sea and its unique features at www.bearsbythesea.com.

Kitty stresses that young entrepreneurs who are going online need to be patient. Business does not suddenly take off. It takes three to six months to get established. She also points out that Net entrepreneurs must be willing to learn the technology. She believes the Internet is the future and finds it exciting to be a part of it. Kitty says that at first she didn't know all the opportunities the Internet offered. Since going online with Bears by the Sea, she has started an Internet marketing business, lectured on how to start Internet businesses, and given private instruction on the Internet.

Online Booksellers

Books are decidedly among the most popular items consumers buy online. They are being sold in cyberstores whose only storefront is on the Net as well as those that also have land-based operations. Internet stores range in size from giants selling more than a million titles to small niche stores offering just needlework books. Most land-based bookstores also have stores on the Net. A fierce battle for customers is beginning to rage and is expected to continue as more and more land-based super chains come aboard the Net. In 1996, Barnes & Noble hired a staff of fifty to establish an online business, demonstrating how important it is for bookstores to have a presence on the Internet. The search for customers already extends beyond the United States. Cody's Books, a land-based bookstore in Berkeley, California, for more than forty-five years, has placed ads in the yellow pages in telephone books in Singapore and Japan to entice customers to its online store (www.codysbooks.com).

Bookselling in cyberspace is far more personalized than it is in many land-based bookstores. For example, Amazon.com, the largest online bookstore with more than one million titles, lets customers sign up for personal notification, via E-mail, of the publication dates of new releases by their favorite authors. And Cody's Books features personal book recommendations from its staff, information about store events, and online interviews with authors. In most cyberstores, customers and staff use E-mail to communicate with each other. It's a variation on the tradition of bookseller and customer sharing a dialog about books.

Amazon.com—an Amazon-Sized Bookstore

Amazon.com, founded by former Wall Street executive Jeffrey P. Bezos, has only been online doing business since 1995. By the end of 1997, more than a million people had bought books from the company. In keeping with its namesake river, this online bookstore has become the largest Internet bookseller in the world. Visit the store at www.amazon.com to see the many special features offered, including greeting returning customers by names, providing suggestions of books they might like to read, E-mailing information about new books to them, letting them read and write book reviews, and tracking orders online.

Today, Amazon.com has expanded far beyond selling just books online. The company has become the WalMart of the Net, selling apparel, office products, magazine subscriptions, DVDs, music, videos, electronics, computers, toys and games, cell phones and service, and more.

Point and click on "Join Our Staff" to discover the many positions available at Amazon.com in such departments as customer service, operations, technology, human resources, marketing, finance, and legal. Do you have the skills for positions that interest you? If not, think about how you can get them. To give you an idea of what Amazon.com is looking for in employees, here are condensed descriptions of two positions.

EXECUTIVE ASSISTANT

Job Description: The customer-service team is seeking a strong candidate who is able to work independently as well as in a team environment. In addition to core administrative duties, this position offers the opportunity to manage a variety of projects within the department and occasional international travel.

Qualifications: Good written and oral communication skills are a must. Knowledge of Microsoft Word, Excel, and Power-Point required, plus a bachelor's degree and three or more years of direct experience in an executive support role. This candidate will be a creative problem solver, highly detail-oriented, with superb organizational skills, and able to switch gears at a moment's notice.

SOFTWARE DEVELOPMENT ENGINEER

Job Description: The company is seeking creative and independent engineers to design, build, and maintain the software platform that powers partners' E-commerce websites. This team is responsible for creating new and efficient applications and services that will further enhance the company's ability to provide powerful E-commerce solutions and the best customer experience on the Web.

Qualifications: Individuals interested in this position should have experience in high-performance, reliable systems in a multitiered, distributed environment. Delivery of mission-critical work in C++ is required, as is expertise with high-end transaction-based systems. Candidates must also have a strong computer science background: a bachelor's degree or higher in computer science is required. Experience with C++, Perl, XML, SOAP, and other distributed computing technologies is a plus.

BookServe—the Internet Story of Two Young Entrepreneurs

You do not need to invest millions to start a successful business on the Internet. Brothers Michael and David Mason were in their twenties when they started BookServe in their family's garage with a stake of only $20,000. They are proof that young entrepreneurs willing to work hard, survive for a while without much money, and commit totally to the business can succeed if they have a solid product idea.

Michael and David started thinking about establishing their own business when one was tired of his career as a political consultant and the other was about to graduate from college. They knew something about the book business, as their father had worked in book distribution, and also knew that it was possible to start an Internet business without too much money, as you did not need a physical storefront. After much investigation and consideration of other ideas, the brothers decided to put the databases of one domestic and three international book distributors online and sell books to cybershoppers. Their business would be service driven—focused on getting books to customers as fast as possible. It would also be global, offering international books that are not readily accessible in the United States.

The development team was made up of the brothers and two programmers who were given a percentage of future sales for their work. The programmers created the search engine for the database as well as the back-end work on the website (what you don't see). Michael and David, who had only basic computer skills, learned sufficient programming skills to create most of the front end of the website (what you do see). They also made arrangements with the distributors and secured access to the Internet through a service provider.

Going Online with Their Business. In September 1995, the Mason brothers' business went online, and sales orders were actually received the very first day. The early months were very busy, with twelve-hour days and a lot of work on weekends because the two brothers were doing everything. They pulled orders from their website, placed them with the distributor (three-fourths of a mile away), picked up the orders from the distributor, and packaged and shipped the books the same day. They were also answering E-mail (as they believed it was very important to talk to their customers), updating their site, and handling their financial work. In addition, they were busy publicizing their business by contacting search engines as well as online businesses that might want to link with them. For example, they might contact (by E-mail) a popular woodworking site and explain that they had eighty woodworking books that the other site's customers might want to access. They did not publicize their site through any newsgroups. The brothers, however, discovered that word of mouth does work, with satisfied customers bringing in more customers.

Within eight months, their business was making enough money that Michael and David were able to start paying themselves. A little more than a year after the business went online, they hired two college students to work part-time handling E-mail and whatever else needed doing. In this small company, everybody had to do everything. As business grew, they also hired an employee to handle general management chores, including ordering supplies and working with shipping companies; a director of systems to update the website and work with publishers; and a director of operations to manage customer service, shipping, and ordering. The brothers served as principals overseeing the business. With success, they were able to cut back on their work hours and no longer work on Sundays. In the fourth quarter of 1996, Ingram Entertainment bought a majority stake in BookServe.

Online Catalog Businesses

For years, many people have done some or all of their shopping through catalogs mailed to their homes. Recently, catalog companies have opened Internet stores—a natural marriage between technology and sales. If you look online, you can find catalogs selling just about everything, from apparel to computers to crafts supplies.

The easiest way to learn more about the successful creation of an online catalog is to look at several. Be sure to look at catalogs from well-known companies such as Lands' End (www.landsend.com), Spiegel (spiegel.com), and L.L. Bean (www.llbean.com). A visit to the Catalog Site at www.catalogsite.com enables you to visit the sites of hundreds of both large and small catalog businesses. You can find even more catalogs by using a search engine to find "online catalog" sites.

Prospective catalog entrepreneurs need to learn such things as how to market a catalog, handle customer service, process orders, and produce an online catalog. You must also pay careful attention to one of the Internet's unique constraints—download time—and avoid placing too many images on a page.

L.L. Bean

Leon Leonwood Bean started a one-man mail-order business in 1912. Today, that business has sales of more than $1 billion and has expanded to forty-five hundred year-round employees. The company focuses on a core business of selling items found in everyone's wardrobe. These are the classics that never go out of style, from jeans to sweaters to men's shirts. This merchandise is sold in retail and outlet stores and online at a website that draws visitors from around the world.

Bean believed that the outdoors and one's ability to experience it are among the greatest gifts the world has to offer. Current employees have many opportunities to use company products as well as the time in the outdoors to enjoy them. Many jobs associated with the Internet are available working with L.L. Bean. Visit http://company.monster.com/llbean to learn more about jobs that are similar to the one in the following Land's End ad for a computer programmer.

SAS PROGRAMMER

Job Description: Land's End is looking for an SAS programmer in our Direct Marketing division to help leverage the wealth of information in our customer database. We're looking for a self-motivated individual who enjoys variety, isn't afraid to multitask, and is ready to take on new challenges.

Qualifications: To be successful in this position, you must have the following knowledge, skills, and abilities:

- Three or more years of programming experience
- Advanced SAS and SQL programming experience
- Experience with UNIX, IBM mainframe
- Experience working with large databases
- Bachelor's or associate degree in business or other quantitative discipline (mathematics, statistics) or equivalent work experience
- Demonstrated ability to work both independently and in teams
- Prefer direct marketing experience

Are You Prepared to Become a Successful Online Entrepreneur?

Just as the forty-niners rushed to California to pan for gold, hundreds of entrepreneurs were rushing aboard the Internet each week before the glow of the Internet diminished. Many never found the success that they anticipated; nevertheless, most experts believe there is still opportunity online for savvy E-commerce merchants. Will you be one of the entrepreneurs who discovers online gold? You have read the stories of several successful online entrepreneurs. Consider now whether you are prepared to start a successful online business or use the Net to enhance the sales of an existing product.

1. You have chosen a product that is a good match with the demographics of online buyers.
2. You have an understanding of how to direct potential online customers to your website.
3. You understand how to use advertising in marketing your website.
4. You are willing to take the time to develop a solid business plan.
5. You understand how an attractive and appealing website is constructed.
6. You have a good general understanding of how the Internet works.
7. You know how to choose the right experts (financial, technical, marketing) to help you develop your business.
8. You understand that you must offer something beyond your product—such as helpful information, contests, or advice—that brings customers repeatedly to your site.
9. You realize that once you get your cyberstore open it will need to be updated constantly.
10. You are willing to make a strong commitment of time and effort to your online business.

Are You Prepared to Work for an E-Commerce Business?

As the Internet takes its first steps beyond infancy, the opportunities are growing for you to find a job with large E-commerce firms. Not only are most big-name retailers establishing an online presence, but many smaller firms are becoming part of larger ones as well. All of these companies require individuals with a wide variety of skills to sell their products online.

For example, large online retailers have jobs in the following areas:

- business and merchant development
- distribution
- editorial
- finance
- human resources
- legal
- marketing
- merchandising
- program management
- software development
- systems engineering
- website development

Most smaller online retailers also have the need for some help in their businesses. Much of this work is part-time or for hire for special projects. Visit online retailers' employment websites to get a picture of what skills are most in demand.

Looking Ahead

At present, few online businesses are making their owners rich. Nevertheless, there is room to be optimistic. The number of online shoppers continues to expand as cybersurfers become more comfortable with online shopping. Shoppers are becoming less reluctant to use their credit cards online because of new security measures. And in the future, new payment systems will emerge, making it just as easy to buy online as it is to drive through toll-pass systems on freeways. Plus, as E-commerce merchants learn more about their customers' shopping habits, online stores will be able to increase sales by catering more to customer preferences. Online sales will also increase when more shoppers have the ability to buy things by clicking on items on their television screens. In addition, merchants will be increasingly able to contact shoppers over their cell phones or PDAs to offer them special products, coupons, or discounts. While Internet commerce now has only a miniscule share of the giant retail trade, some estimates suggest that it could have as much as 10 percent of total sales after 2010. At this point, E-commerce will have become an important part of retail sales with many job opportunities.

CHAPTER NINE

Education, Media, Research, and Other Online Careers

The list of Internet-related careers is growing at an astronomical rate. More and more common activities are migrating online. Instead of going to high school, college, or a trade school, many students are now going online for their education. And those too pressed for time to read a daily newspaper are acquiring the habit of reading online newspapers throughout the day. And for recreational reading, there now are online magazines, or E-zines, and E-books. Local, state, and federal governments are moving to the Internet to let you handle activities from paying taxes to applying for permits online. Every one of these activities translates into jobs for cybersurfers eager to turn their obsession with cyberspace into full- or part-time jobs. Whenever you go aboard the Net, keep your eyes open for more career possibilities and be sure to research Net job trends.

Education Careers

One terrific benefit of the Internet is that it has made learning far more convenient for so many people. Instead of having to travel to a class that is given at a specific time, students of all ages can now choose to take courses on just about anything, whenever they want and wherever they have access to a computer. The age of the virtual classroom has arrived, bringing online career possibilities for those who want to teach and for those who want to provide support services.

Online College Education

It has become possible for students to complete college without ever setting foot on campus. Some, however, attend what are known as hybrid programs, which combine classroom and online instruction. Two leading universities in online instruction are the University of Maryland University College (www.umuc.edu/gen/virtuniv.html) and the University of Phoenix (www.uophx.edu). At most colleges, the courses are tailored for working adults, with the most popular offerings in business administration, accounting, information systems, human resource management, and marketing. Some colleges also offer noncredit courses for cybersurfers to pursue their interests in such topics as World War II, the Westward Movement, and art history. And colleges are beginning to offer online courses to high school students.

Students enroll and order their books online, use E-mail to communicate with their teachers and fellow students, post messages on bulletin boards for other students, chat in real time with their teachers and classmates, download materials from the course's online library, and do research using Internet resources. Students don't usually have to go to colleges or designated testing centers except for final exams.

To deliver online courses, cybercolleges employ teachers as well as technical and administrative staff. Teachers for online programs are typically faculty members from the source institution or other colleges and specialists in business and professional fields. They are selected for their interest in working individually with students at a distance. These teachers must write course materials, and to do so they must have an understanding of what it is technically possible to present online. They must know how to use E-mail, post notices on bulletin boards, and handle real-time online discussions, as well as be aware of the resources on the Internet that will aid their students. In addition to academic and other specialized staff on the administrative side, there are technical experts responsible for putting the program online. These include instructional designers, graphic designers, programmers, and others who are knowledgeable about the Internet and telecommunications industries.

Cybercollege Job Opportunities. In 2000, the online enrollment of the University of Maryland University College numbered forty thousand students worldwide. It is expected that enrollment will pass one hundred thousand by 2003. Significant increases in enrollment at most online colleges means a boom in jobs for cybersurfers who are interested in education. The ad below provides a condensed description of a job at eCornell, a subsidiary of Cornell University that produces, markets, and delivers online professional and educational programs developed in conjunction with Cornell University's schools and colleges.

MARKETING DESIGNER AND PROGRAMMER

Job Description: Work in a fast-paced, collaborative environment to design and develop marketing materials ranging from E-mails and banners to multifunctional stand-alone and integrated Web pages. Involved in all areas of the production; focused on concept design, development, and execution.

Qualifications:
- Experience in designing and developing marketing material. Portfolio required.
- An understanding of usability principles.
- In-depth experience with HTML, JSP, Photoshop, Illustrator and/or Freehand, JavaScript, Flash, and website development tools such as Dreamweaver, Image Ready, and Fireworks.
- Must be comfortable and efficient using new technologies in a dynamic environment.

- Must be able to work on multiple projects at a time and work well within a collaborative team environment.
- Minimum two years of experience designing commercial websites.
- Educational background in a related field, such as graphic design, publishing, multimedia, or equivalent work.
- Bachelor's degree and at least two years of Web design experience required. Please provide a portfolio of example URLs.

Community College Workshop Teacher

Early in the Internet era, Lorrita Ford, a community college librarian, realized that the Net would be a useful tool for gathering and disseminating information. She learned how to navigate on the Net by reading books, attending workshops, and subscribing to several listservs (Internet mailing lists). In 1993, she began to teach formal workshops to faculty and staff members. Within a year, she created a formal one-unit Internet course and incorporated the Internet into traditional print and electronic research courses. In 1997 she began developing a three-unit course on information competency and literacy, which included using the Internet. Internet classes are now part of the community college research skills curriculum.

A Public School Instructor

Dale Beasley teaches an HTML class to middle school students as part of an elective program. The students have in turn created their own Web pages, which are included in the school's website. Dale has his own flatbed scanner at home, which he uses to scan student pictures and art to upload to the school's Web page. The hardest thing about his job has been convincing the teachers and students to contribute items so their Web pages remain viable and current. On the other hand, he has enjoyed helping other teachers set up their own schools' Web pages, including one college instructor in Sydney, Australia.

Elementary School Technology Resource Specialist

Andy Poon was an experienced elementary school teacher with a bachelor's and two master's degrees in education when his principal asked him to supervise the installation of technological upgrades at his school through the state's modernization program. This was in the mid-1990s when schools were purchasing new computers and wiring their classrooms for the Internet. Andy had two unique qualifications for this position. He was a computer buff whose first and second grade students had been working on computers since the late eighties. Because of his tech savvy and resourcefulness, Andy was able to put together a primitive computer lab with the one school-provided computer and a few donated computers. The students were taught basic keyboard skills, word processing, and skill drill programs that were available at the time. His second qualification was that he had been attending technology classes after school and received a certificate from the state attesting to his knowledge of computers.

In his job as a technology resource specialist, Andy oversaw the implementation of more than a hundred computers schoolwide, complete wiring for Internet access in each classroom, and development of the school's technology plan. He was in charge of the school's in-house repair and maintenance department. He also taught beginning computer classes to the students and worked with teachers to integrate technology into their classrooms.

While Andy's initial assignment to this position was for six months, he is still working at this job, which has changed as the school acquired more computers and new equipment has been introduced. Today, due to the lack of classroom space, he is in charge of a mobile laptop computer lab with wireless printing and

Internet access. An important part of his assignment is offering professional development to his fellow teachers. Once a month, he holds a workshop instructing them in the latest technological advances. Andy also makes a brief presentation at monthly faculty meetings.

Career Advice from Andy. If you have an interest in technology and want to work in public schools, get a teaching credential first for the level you wish to teach. Then take courses that will certify you to teach technology classes. Demand is high for teachers with these qualifications.

Teaching Courses on Using the Internet

If you are an adept cybersurfer, you can smoothly hop aboard the Net and surf for the information you want or explore new territory. There still are, however, a great number of people who are clueless about how to navigate the Internet. For these people, words such as *browser, search engine, modem,* and *domain* are a foreign language. In order to take advantage of all the Internet offers, Net neophytes need instruction. At the same time, there are people who want to put material aboard the Internet but need instruction in more advanced areas such as designing Web pages, marketing websites, or working with HTML and virtual reality modeling language (VRML). Others simply want to know how to use the Net for researching, shopping, or socializing. Furthermore, an enormous number of students in recently wired schools need to know how to use the Internet for educational purposes. Because the Internet is not static but constantly growing and changing, each evolution spawns a dozen other changes. For this reason alone, there will always be careers in teaching Internet skills.

People needing to know more about using the Internet typically acquire the requisite skills from reading books, hiring trainers, attending classes, or talking to knowledgeable users. Community colleges, university extension programs, public schools, professional training companies, computer stores, public libraries, and many websites offer a variety of Internet training classes and need instructors to teach these classes. Except for public school instructors, who need teacher certification, the major job qualification for Internet instructors is to have solid online and communication skills. If being an Internet instructor interests you, get your feet wet by serving as a volunteer in a library program designed to teach patrons about the Internet. Most Internet teaching jobs at the present time are part-time positions. Instructors may be paid by the courses they teach or the hours they work.

Personal Internet Instructor. You don't have to wait until you graduate from college or even high school to become an Internet instructor if you are an expert cybersurfer. Joshua Joseph Soros started giving both adults and children lessons on using computers and surfing the Net when he was in seventh grade. Although he was largely self-taught, Joshua did take some children's computer classes and worked with a neighbor who is a computer graphics designer. As he gained expertise, children and adults began asking him to teach them, so he started a business teaching computer classes to individual learners. His only advertising was word-of-mouth and a listing on the local ISP's website.

Joshua enjoyed teaching others how to surf the Net, whether they wanted to do research or just have fun. His students learned how to use the Internet to do such things as check their stocks, investigate the weather around the country, and reserve books at the local library. He also wanted to see people his age experiment and have fun on the Internet in order to prepare for future online jobs. Joshua continued teaching his computer and Internet classes until schoolwork intruded, and he no longer had the time for a part-time job. Today, he is enrolled in college and using the computer in all of his classes.

More Online Teaching Opportunities

Browse around the Internet, and you will quickly discover that it is a regular schoolhouse, with courses offered in such subjects as photography, genealogy, Web page design, becoming a United States citizen, word processing, cooking, and writing a novel. These courses may just be for a single session or may last for several weeks. Use a search engine to discover the many places where "online courses" are offered. Then stop by and visit a few sites and consider whether or not you might like to become an online teacher.

An Online Instructor's Story. First and foremost, Blythe Camenson is an author with fifty nonfiction books to her credit. She is also a director of the Fiction Writer's Connection (www .fictionwriters.com), writes a newsletter for the association, and provides a critiquing service and advice for members. It is with this background that she approached a large Internet service provider and asked about teaching online. She proposed a course called "How to Approach Editors and Agents" and was soon teaching the course online. After two years, she added another course, "How to Write Winning Query Letters." A background in computers was not necessary for this job, nor was a teaching degree required. It was important, however, to have a good command of her subject area and the ability to communicate well in an online environment. It also helped to be a fast and accurate typist.

Blythe's classes were held in live sessions. Each student sat at home in front of his or her own computer and joined others in a live classroom. As the instructor, Blythe lectured a little, held question-and-answer sessions, brought guest speakers to class (such as agents and editors), and made material available to students in the server's online library. Even though each class was only two hours a week for four or six weeks, the number of hours spent outside the classroom were almost uncountable. Blythe had lessons to prepare, registrations to keep track of, material to upload to the library, and the bulletin board to monitor. Furthermore, instructors were expected to sign on early before class and stay online late after class. Blythe also spent a lot of time with E-mail both before and during each term. Potential students had questions about her courses, which involved sending them class and registration information, and current students often needed help downloading materials and even finding their way to class.

Right now, for most instructors, online education only offers part-time employment opportunities, just as many live classrooms in adult education settings do. Blythe was paid for each student in her classes. At that time, several years ago, she received only $15 per student for her four-week course and $21.25 per student for the six-week course. There were also eight-week and twelve-week classes that paid a little more. You should expect this position to pay slightly better today. In addition to teaching, Blythe enjoyed free service from the server. Word-of-mouth brought her new students each term, and there were always repeat students. But to get a good class size, she had to spend time promoting her course online.

Although compensation for her time was very low, Blythe worked as an instructor because she loved being able to help new writers avoid costly mistakes and found it exciting meeting people from all over the country. She even had students from Europe attend her classes. For her, one of the biggest benefits of being an online instructor was being able to teach a course from her home. After several years, Blythe stopped being an online instructor for the server to concentrate on her writing and teach E-mail courses for writers for Fiction Writer's Connection. In this way, she is still involved as an online instructor.

A Look at Salaries in Education

The news is good for prospective teachers at the K–12 level. Strong demand is pushing up salaries. The average salary for all teachers is more than $40,000. While this is an all-time high, it is far short of the salary that professionals in the computer industry enjoy. And the average teaching salary varies enormously state by state. At the college level, salaries are higher in private than public schools. Full-time college professors earn an average salary of more than $76,000 a year; the average for associate professors is above $55,000, and for assistant professors, it is over $45,000. The average salary of college instructors and lecturers is slightly less than that of K–12 teachers.

....

A Look at Online Media

As a seasoned cybersurfer, you probably do much of your newspaper and magazine reading online. This is the current trend, especially in the newspaper market. After the advent of the World Wide Web, hundreds of companies went online to create Web newspapers and magazines, and established newspapers and magazines also put their products online as well. Unfortunately, everyone soon discovered that there was a very limited amount of Web advertising money, an increasing number of competing publishers, and subscribers unwilling to pay for content because they were accustomed to free Web pages. Overblown expectations caused several publications to stop publishing or to scale back on their content. Nevertheless, most newspapers now recognize the importance of being the dominant online news source in their communities. And some online magazines are succeeding because they have found a niche with dedicated readers.

Online Newspapers

The newspaper subscription success story on the Internet is the *Wall Street Journal Interactive Edition*, which had more than fifty thousand paying subscribers as early as 1997. You can tour the subscription site at http://wsj.com/tour. Other newspapers, however, have found that they can only charge for their electronic back files, advertisements, and help-wanted ads; they are earnestly seeking ways to entice readers to pay for online news and other features. Recently, several newspapers have made users register before entering their websites. This data is then used for a fee by advertisers hoping to reach a specified group of consumers. Because of the advertising payoff, more newspapers are expected to raise registration firewalls. Although the immediate future may not be entirely rosy, every newspaper that has an online presence also has full- or at least part-time jobs involving the editorial and technical sides of putting a paper online. Some have quite large staffs.

Career Advice from a Senior Online Editor. Donna Yannish was the senior online editor for the online version of the *San Jose Mercury News* when it was launched in 1994. According to Donna, the base of a job in online publishing for a news organization is good news-gathering skills. This is a relatively new medium, but as with the older media, content is key. Young people interested in online publishing should use the medium—and other news outlets as well. Read, watch, and listen to all you can online. Embrace the Internet as well as the other news outlets. Journalism school is a great way to learn news-gathering techniques and develop good news judgment. Schools are beginning to teach specifics for online publishing.

Online-Only News Organizations

Newspapers, magazines, and radio and television networks are not the only news sources on the Internet. The Web is loaded with sites promising to bring you the latest news. *CNET News.com* at www.news.com, is a twenty-four-hour-a-day technology news service covering the computer industry and the Internet. In addition to providing about forty original stories every day, the site offers links to interesting stories in other publications, weekly columns by some of the editors, and interviews of leading technology figures. The more than forty-five members of the editorial staff are mostly experienced journalists from newspapers and magazines. Go to the website to see how the news is presented and for job information. Other news services include: Yahoo! News at www.news.yahoo.com and Microsoft's venture with NBC at www.msnbc.com.

News Editor at *CNET News.com*. You don't wait for the presses to stop when you are news editor at *CNET News.com*. It has round-the-clock breaking technology news coverage, features, and special reports on technology's impact on enterprise computing, E-business, finance, communications, personal technology, and entertainment. Scott Ard, the news editor, assigns stories in work sessions running from 8:30 A.M. to 7:00 P.M. along with frequent weekend and night stints on the job. It is essential for Scott and his staff to work as quickly as possible to meet breaking news deadlines, which require the posting of thirty or so stories a day. Handling this job requires Scott to go on the Internet to check competitors' sites, do research, stay on top of the *CNET News.com* site, and read editorials. Recently, Scott became managing editor and has the increased responsibility of doing more planning and production work.

Internet Magazines

Since the first days of the Internet, there have been magazines on the Net. Most are published by individuals and don't usually carry ads. Today, there are tens of thousands of magazines on every topic under the sun on the Internet. You will also find that major Net print magazine publishers such as *Internet Magazine* (www.internet-magazine.com) and *Online* (www.onlinemag.net) also have online magazines as well as such well-known magazines as *Time, Business Week,* and *People.* One of the best-known Web-only launch efforts is Microsoft's *Slate* (www.slate.msn.com). It is an interactive magazine of politics, policy, and culture. Because of the reluctance of subscribers to pay for online publications, there is no fee for *Slate.*

Online magazines employ staffs similar to those of online newspapers. If the magazine is associated with a print publication, the editorial staff is primarily involved in adding Web enhancements to articles. However, staff on a publication that is only online will have the responsibility of creating original copy, as does the staff of print publications. When you visit the websites of magazines, be sure to look at the staff and job opening pages to see what types of editorial and technical jobs are available.

ONLINE—a Print and Net Magazine. *ONLINE: The Leading Magazine for Information Professionals* is a print magazine that also has selected articles on its website at www.onlinemag.net. The magazine is written for information professionals—the people who do in-depth research primarily for businesses, using such tools as the Internet, database systems, and CD-ROMs. You'll learn more about this career later on in the chapter.

As editor of both the print and Net versions of *ONLINE*, Marydee Ojala has these major responsibilities:

- planning content
- finding authors for articles
- managing publication agreements with authors
- editing all articles
- approving all graphics
- writing a monthly column
- putting selected articles on the Net website

Marydee's job is a good one for cybersurfers as she has to go online to check the facts in every article. This involves visiting many websites. Plus, she does all her research online using the free Internet as well as fee-based research services.

Although there are no entry-level positions at *ONLINE*, many magazines do have the starting position of assistant editor. If you aspire to be an editor, you might want to start by becoming an occasional feature author. Then, as you build a reputation, you may be able to become a regular columnist and, finally, an editor. Alternatively, you might consider editing a newsletter on a volunteer basis, possibly for your professional association, church, or school. Although you won't be paid, you'll have a product to show potential employers.

Marydee's career with *ONLINE* began in a rather interesting way. While she was a corporate librarian at a large multinational bank, she and two fellow librarians wrote a letter to the editor commenting on an article that had been published in the first issue of *ONLINE*. Unbelievably, the publisher came from Connecticut to San Francisco to talk to them about their viewpoint and asked if they were interested in writing. Only Marydee was, and she wrote an article that was published in the second volume of the magazine.

After writing some other feature stories, Marydee became a regular columnist. Even after establishing her own research business and during a stint in Europe, she kept writing for the magazine, building a solid reputation. When the editor of *Database*, a sister publication, resigned, Marydee applied for the job and got it. Two years later, she switched jobs with the editor of *ONLINE*, as it was a better fit for her background.

Career Advice from Marydee. "The most important course in school for me was eighth grade English, where the teacher drummed basic grammar into us. I have both a bachelor's and a master's degree, but it is eighth grade English that I fall back on in my work as an editor.

"Do you need a degree in journalism to be a successful editor? Some publications require that as an entry-level requirement. For much of the trade press, which is how *ONLINE* is characterized, in-depth knowledge of the industry is equally important."

Computer Gaming World. Gamesters do not spend all of their time online. They also spend time reading about games, game technology, and ratings of new games in magazines like *Computer Gaming World* (www.computergaming.com). Staffs are small at these magazines. The jobs are in the editorial, art, and production departments and at the copy desk. There are also intern positions. And most employees have more than one responsibility. As review editor at *Computer Gaming World*, Robert Coffey selects freelance reviewers to review from twelve to more than twenty games for each issue. He edits the reviews and also writes news, reviews, previews, and the back-page column. Robert describes his job as a game-playing job because he and the other editors play a number of games to check that they agree with the reviewers' ratings of the quality of the games. To him the best way for getting a job with a magazine is to work as an intern.

A Look at Online Media Salaries

As the number of online publications increases, the demand for writers, editors, and technical staff is also increasing. At the same time, there is considerable competition for these jobs. The average medium salary for print magazine editors is above $40,000 and for newspaper editors above $37,000. Online salaries are comparable. Writers earn less, but technical experts may earn more. Those who elect to freelance are not usually highly paid. They may be paid by the word ($1.00 per word) but are more commonly paid by the page (up to $300 per page) or article (from $300 to $1,000). Experienced writers with solid reputations earn more.

Writing About and for the Internet

The recent explosion of writing about the Internet offers a great number of cybersurfers the opportunity to have careers as writers. Visit the computer section of a bookstore and you will quickly discover a great number of new books on the Internet. Especially popular are books on how to use the Internet and how to make money on the Internet. Besides writing for online media publications, look for opportunities in computer magazines that now have columns and articles on the Internet discussing just about every aspect of the Net, from online security to instant Internet access to Web marketing tips.

Think also of all of the printed material on each Web page that you visit. Someone had to create that material. Chances are it was created by a freelance writer or someone at a company involved in the creation of Web pages.

Writing is a competitive field in which experience counts. An excellent way to get this experience is by writing for high school, college, and community papers and doing reviews of websites.

A Freelance Writer in the Online Age

Through more than sixty books, Alfred Glossbrenner has introduced more than one million people to the wonders of computers in general and the Internet in particular. The hallmark of his work is an uncanny ability to explain high technology in a way that absolutely anyone can understand. His wife, Emily, who has close to twenty years of experience in computers and marketing, has collaborated with him on numerous bestselling computer books.

Since graduating from Princeton University in 1972, Alfred has been a full-time freelance writer, editor, book packager, and magazine columnist. Prior to 1979 he had written five how-to sports books. But that year he encountered what was then called a *dedicated word processor*. It turned out that the machine could not only produce text, it could also "go online," a feat that was quite rare at the time. After half an hour of exploring the Source, an early online service, Alfred was hooked forever.

In the years since, Alfred has written extensively about specific online systems, about "how to look it up online," and about the Internet and World Wide Web. He has also written extensively about shareware, DOS, Windows 3.1, and hard disk drives.

Before the Glossbrenners decided to concentrate on other areas of writing, they typically wrote a book in approximately four to six weeks, frequently putting in twelve- to fourteen-hour days. They followed a total-immersion approach that yielded a book containing the most current information available when the book went to press. There are exceptions, of course, but the typical computer book earns about $15,000 to $20,000 and has a fairly short shelf life (six to twelve months), so it's important to be able to turn books out quickly.

Today, Emily spends most of her time indexing computer books while Alfred works on a variety of projects usually associated with the Net. He has written the scripts for 150 career videos for high school students that were put online and distributed as CDs. Alfred has also written the scripts for Web-based training for several companies. Plus, he frequently writes the copy for websites.

Career Advice from Alfred. "If you decide to become a free-lance writer, you will find the easiest way to get jobs is from past associations and your reputation. You are not likely to find the job you want on job boards."

··

Information Brokers—Internet Supersearchers

Being an information broker is a relatively new career, as are the tools that are now being used to handle a great part of this job—the Internet and online services. What information brokers do is gather information for clients, often businesses, from a wide variety of resources, for a fee. While print was once the major information resource for information brokers, they are now spending much of their time online using commercial database services, published resources on the Internet, E-mail, listservs, and newsgroups. Information brokers may be self-employed or work for companies offering research services in a variety of fields. Many have been trained as librarians. The average hourly rate for brokers running an information business is between $75 and $200.

An excellent source of information about this profession is the Association of Independent Information Professionals website at www.aiip.org. One of the many membership benefits is matching new members with more experienced members who give them advice on how to grow their businesses. You can find books on super searchers in this profession and on running a successful research business at http://books.infotoday.com.

An Information Broker's Career Story

Mary Ellen Bates is the principal of Bates Information Services, a research and consulting business based in Washington, D.C., that she started in 1991. She provides business research services to business professionals and corporate librarians and consulting services to the online industry and independent information professionals. Here are examples of the kinds of research she does:

- the impact of information technology on the global economy
- the outlook for the pre-fab housing industry in Europe and Japan
- recent high-tech developments in the grocery industry
- joint ventures in the "edutainment" field

As an information broker, Mary Ellen uses online databases and the Internet as well as such resources as trade associations and government agencies. While she has been using online research-type databases since 1979, she only started using the Internet in 1992, when she enrolled in a two-day introductory course because she was getting nowhere fast trying to teach herself how to use the Net. Today, she feels at home with the contents of the Internet and has developed a good sense of how valid the information is. She must understand the bias of every source.

A Day with Mary Ellen. A quick look at one of Mary Ellen's days shows that being an information broker is not a nine-to-five job. At the start of this day, she reviews and responds to her E-mail and reads postings from ten E-mail discussion groups she subscribes to. Then she settles down to the work of the day. Mary Ellen is in the middle of a project that requires her to access professional online services for information and then the U.S. Patent and Trademark Office database, followed by a visit to a few of the market research aggregators on the Web. Once she has all the material from her searches, she refines and organizes it for her client. Since it is the end of the month, she next takes the time to do her monthly invoices and pay her bills. At 11:00 A.M., Mary Ellen receives a phone call from a colleague with an online search request. After a quick walk with her dogs, she begins to do some serious Web surfing for another client followed by a run in the nearby park with a friend. Back in the office again, she checks to see how the work is going with a telephone researcher who is doing some work for one of her clients. The next hour is spent on another project before she pulls out folders to work on a speech she will be giving. When it's close to the end of the day, Mary Ellen talks to a new information broker she is mentoring. Finally, it's time for the day to end, so she starts her backup program, which saves all new files onto a Zip disk, and packs up some professional reading that she might do in the evening.

A Deep-Sea Diver. Mary Ellen generally considers herself a deep-sea diver rather than a cybersurfer, as she usually searches for in-depth information rather than skimming the surface looking for the next wave. She goes to sites that she knows and trusts because she has found reliable information there before. For example, if Mary Ellen were to get a question about travel to Albania, she would go straight to the Department of State website because she knows that the State Department keeps travelers' advisories there. She does, however, become a cybersurfer when she is doing patent research because she has to look all over the Net for any prior mention of a possible new invention.

Much of Mary Ellen's effort to stay current with general trends in her profession—as well as to learn about new sites—is done online. She subscribes to several library/information professional listservs and reads all the Internet material in *ONLINE, Searcher, Information Advisor, Cyberskeptic,* and *Econtent.* Plus, she finds that there is a lot of information in professional-oriented E-zines. Before owning her own company, Mary Ellen, who has a master's degree in library and information science, worked as a law librarian and corporate library manager for about fifteen years. To learn even more about Mary Ellen's work and professional activities, visit her website at www.batesinfo.com. There, you will discover that she has also written six books relating to Internet research and speaks several times a month on this topic in places ranging from Arizona to Australia.

Career Advice from Mary Ellen. Mary Ellen believes that there will be a continuing need for information professionals as more and more people discover how difficult it is to access the information they want quickly. Besides taking courses in business because they will be running a business, she feels that one of the most helpful things prospective information brokers can do is to join the Association of Independent Information Professionals (www.aiip.org).

Working for the Government Online

At the federal, state, and local levels, government agencies are jumping aboard the Internet to offer information and services to citizens. You can download tax forms, find out about licensing fees and zoning regulations, read the notes on city council meetings, communicate easily with public officials—including the president of the United States—by E-mail. You can do more each day as an increasing number of government units come online. This activity creates a tremendous need for government employees as well as consultants who know their way around the Internet. You can find out about jobs with the federal government online at the U.S. Office of Personnel Management website at www.usajobs.opm .gov.search.html. Go to the "First Timers Start Here" page to learn how to apply for jobs and find your ideal job. If you are set on working for a particular agency, visit that agency's website or, if convenient, visit the local offices of the agency for more job information. For state and local government employment service agencies, visit the website of the state or locality where you are seeking employment.

A Job with the U.S. Department of Education

All of Peter Kickbush's professional jobs have been with the U.S. Department of Education. His current job title is policy analyst; however, he spends 80 to 90 percent of his time using the Internet. Peter and his colleague Kirk Winters research, write, and edit a listserv called EDInfo, which produces two to three messages a week about recent Department of Education studies, publications, reports, and funding opportunities. He also contributes to the department's website. Initially, he was responsible for HTML markup, but now he serves as a consultant to others within the department who are contemplating putting their information online. Peter works with individuals who range from external website contract managers to internal education policy makers.

The greatest challenge in his job is keeping up—not just with the furious pace with which new technologies hit the market, but also with the needs of the department's customers and with modifying the systems to meet those needs. Peter believes that the Internet is redefining how the government interacts with citizens, and he finds it exciting to be part of shaping this redefinition.

Working in Libraries in the Information Age

Rapid changes in technology have brought computers into libraries. Many libraries now offer patrons the opportunity to use the information sources available on the Internet, which means librarians have to be Net savvy. Part of a reference librarian's job has become cybersurfing—going aboard the Internet to evaluate search engines and content and look for good links. Librarians are also turning into webmasters and website builders. And research librarians are spending a great part of their days online searching the Web to answer patrons' questions.

Your Internet Career Can Change

Many cybersurfers and online types have found that their careers have evolved organically in this fast-paced information revolution because new opportunities are constantly appearing. Reva Basch, who has been involved with online activities since the early 1980s, is an excellent example of how careers can evolve. She began her online career, long before the advent of the Web, as a researcher at a pioneering independent research company where she learned to use online research services, such as DIALOG and LEXISNexis, and ended up as the company's vice president and director of research. Her next move was to the technical side in 1986, when she went to work for Mead Data Central (now LEXISNexis) designing front-end software for the NEXIS search service. Then in 1988, she started her own firm, Aubergine Information Services, which provided online research on just about any topic. Her business has evolved over the years, expanding to include writing and editing, speaking, and consulting.

Reva has written four books, all dealing with online information and research. She is the executive editor for the Super Searchers book series published by Information Today. Reva has also written hundreds and hundreds of articles and columns. She wrote the *Compleat Searcher* column for the late *Online User* magazine and was the *Cybernaut* columnist for *Computer Life* magazine. From 1998 through 2000, she wrote the column *Reva's (W)rap* for *ONLINE* magazine. As a speaker on such Net topics as "Delusions of Adequacy? Supersearchers Versus the Net" and "Measuring Our Research Skills in the Internet Age," Reva has traveled throughout the United States and to Europe, Australia, and Canada. She also consults with companies in the information business, helping them design better and more useable databases and online services, and she has embarked on teaching a Web-based course in advanced online searching for a graduate school in library science.

Reva works alone and at home, determining her own schedule and work rhythm. She has access to the Internet via a high-speed satellite connection. For a break between projects or in the midst of one, this online aficionado goes online to socialize, and she always travels with a laptop. You can learn more about Reva's very satisfying online career and life by visiting her home page at www.well.com/user/reva.

More Job Areas to Explore

So many jobs now have tie-ins with the Internet. Doctors go online to access health-care information, consult with other doctors, communicate with patients, take online courses, and keep electronic medical records. Law libraries are rapidly being replaced with commercial databases, and more and more lawyers are using the NET to find primary legal materials. Tax preparers find forms on the Net and file more and more returns online every year. A minister downloads a sermon from the Internet to use with his congregation. Thousands of company employees work from home using the Internet to reach their companies. Fast-food and take-out restaurant workers receive orders over the Internet. All advertising and marketing people now have to consider the Net in the promotion and sales of products. In the future, you can expect most jobs to have some association with the Net, which is great news for cybersurfers and other online types who will be able to combine avocation and vocation in the workplace.

CHAPTER TEN

The Internet and Future Opportunities

When electricity was first discovered, no one could have guessed how it would revolutionize everyone's life. It was the same story with the invention of the telephone and television. Today, the new kid in technology is the Internet. No one can come close to guessing what it will be like and what new Net job opportunities will emerge in five, ten, or a hundred years from now. Without question, cybersurfers and other online types, you are in the very early days of a communications revolution that will have a tremendous impact on lives, jobs, and companies—an impact that we've only begun to feel.

On the horizon, as more and more people come aboard the Internet and its capabilities increase, the vision is emerging of a world where you can communicate with anyone, anywhere, at any time, and even see and hear that person. It's a world where millions of bits of information will be literally at your fingertips. And it's a world with video on demand, convenient online shopping, online education, digital documents replacing paper documents, news delivered interactively, low-overhead electronic banks, virtual-reality (three-dimensional) "worlds" that you can explore, businesses working with other businesses online, and more than you can ever imagine. The Internet hasn't even scratched the surface of its potential, especially in education and business. Some hot areas that you might like to explore include:

- broadband Internet
- customized E-mail
- Internet cafés
- multiplayer online gaming
- voice over Internet service
- wireless Internet

This communications revolution is moving so fast that the Internet is different every few months. You are in the midst of historic change. At the same time, as a cybersurfer who is fascinated by the Net, you have the opportunity to contribute to the evolution of the Internet through the career you select. Improved technology is needed. You could be one of the many who will find technical breakthroughs. Businesspeople, professionals, and educators who understand the new technology are needed to help bring the Internet into people's homes, schools, and workplaces. You could be one of them.

Predictions from the Pros

Predicting the future is always difficult. Few saw the dot-com bust occurring. Surprises inevitably occur. Nevertheless, it should be helpful for cybersurfers beginning to plan their Net careers to see what prominent players in the cyberworld think about where job opportunities and the Internet will be in the next few years.

John Levine—Author of *The Internet for Dummies*

"Network security is clearly a growth area, particularly since Microsoft, the dominant vendor, seems unable to produce software that doesn't require weekly updates to plug its many holes. Security is a large field, ranging from technical network issues to setting and managing company security and privacy policies to compliance with data privacy laws, the last particularly for companies that do business in Europe.

"Web design per se (just creating pretty Web pages) is no longer much of a business, but people who combine knowledge of Web-building tools and databases will have plenty of work, as will people with skills in putting together multimedia that work on the Web.

"And there's still plain-old network management—keeping someone's corner of the Net running. As the corners get bigger and the demands put on them grow, the job of making it all work can be surprisingly complex."

Margaret Riley Dikel—Net Consultant and Creator of *The Riley Guide*

"One thing to note is that when I began doing my work on the Internet, it was still in relative infancy compared to what it is now. I am self-taught and learned on the job. Today, that's not good enough. You have to have credentials. The world realizes that programmers are not the best information managers, so librarians and editors are usually in control of the content of the Web servers. However, you must have demonstrated experience in this area, and building your own website isn't enough. You must have formal training, maybe even certification. I had a university website plus my own popular public site behind me, along with a reputation as someone who could not only divide the good from the bad but also design a user-friendly way for people to navigate through a site. That is a reputation built over more than ten years in this field."

Peter Kickbush—Policy Analyst, U.S. Department of Education

"I've never been very good at predicting, but in the future, I think jobs on the Internet will be hard to discern. Everyone will be using it for everything. So my advice to young people would be to diversify yourself. Without a doubt, double major in college—one major in computer science or engineering, the other in business or the humanities. Take logic and philosophy courses. Learn about the technology, but don't be seduced by the notion that technology in and of itself is the answer. Think of technology and the Internet as the vessel that carries information. I think people who will successfully exploit the overwhelming potential of the Internet are those who understand both the vessel and the information. Individuals who use this incredible tool to communicate meaningful information and ideas will find jobs on the Internet."

Reva Basch—Cybernaut Columnist, Author, and Net Consultant

"From a librarian's perspective, the Internet desperately needs better indexes and search tools. The Web is in the process of becoming ubiquitous, the platform for all sorts of information exchange and communication into the foreseeable future, and the possibilities are virtually unlimited."

Egil Juliussen—President of *Computer Industry Almanac*

"Eventually, the Internet will emulate all present-day communications functions. In the distribution of information, the Net will have the capability of the telephone, radio, television, newspapers, and magazines. Plus it will add many new functions. At the present time, the Internet is rather like a vast library with all its books on the floor. Individuals will be needed in library-type jobs to bring order to this chaos or the Internet will not live up to its potential."

Keeping Up with What's Happening on the Internet

Dedicated cybersurfers and other online types, your passion for the Internet is what will keep you informed about changes on the Net that could affect your career. As you become more and more knowledgeable about the Internet, bookmark those sites that offer solid information about what is happening on the Internet so that you can easily visit them again and again. Visit the home pages of Internet magazines and newspapers frequently to look for career and technology information. Check what is happening at companies such as Microsoft, Amazon.com, eBay, and America Online—leading players in the Internet world. Everything that you need to know about choosing an Internet or online career is on the Internet. Enjoy your cybersurfing!

Glossary

ADSL   Asymmetric digital subscriber line; subscriber line that allows you to receive more data than with an ISDN line but limits what you can send back. ADSL uses POTS (plain old telephone service) and may become one of the most popular choices in the next few years.

ARPANET   The forerunner of the Internet, developed by the Department of Defense in the late sixties and early seventies.

ASCII   American Standard for Computer Information Interchange; plain text characters that can be read by almost any program. Pronounced "ask-key."

Applets   Small downloadable Java applications that can be run from a Web page.

Backbone   A high-speed line that forms a major pathway within a network or links one complete network with another.

Bandwidth   A measure of the amount of information you can send through a connection.

Baud   The speed at which modems transfer data, listed in bps (bytes per second), kbps (kilobytes per second), or Mbps (megabits per second).

Broadband   Generally used to mean a fast connection.

Browser   Software used to surf the Web.

Cable modem   Provides Internet access by using part of the bandwidth on a cable TV connection.

CGI   Common Gateway Interface; a programming language used by most Web servers for handling forms.

CTI   Computer telephony integration; the convergence of computer and telephone technologies.

Cybercash   A method of real-time credit card processing.

Cybermall   A collection of business Web pages offered online by one Web access provider, often anchored by a major store.

Domain name   A unique name identifying an Internet site.

Download   Copy a file from a remote system to your computer.

DSL   Digital subscriber line.

E-mail   Electronic mail, used as both a noun and a verb.

Ethernet   A common way to connect computers in a LAN (local-area network).

Encryption   Scrambling a message so that it is difficult or impossible for another person to read. It is increasingly used when transmitting credit card numbers.

Firewall   A method used to protect a network from access by those outside the network, it is designed to provide greater security to a server.

FTP   File transfer protocol; a system allowing files to be transferred from one computer to another via the Internet.

Gopher   A tool for finding and retrieving files on the Internet.

Home page   The main page out of a collection of Web pages, it is also used to mean individuals' or businesses' own websites.

Host   Any computer that can function as the beginning and end point of data transfers.

HTML   Hypertext markup language; a formatting language used to publish hypertext on the World Wide Web.

HTTP   Hypertext transfer protocol; a standardized set of rules for sending hypertext documents on the Web.

Hub   A network-connecting device linking computers, printers, and other devices.

Hypertext   A type of document containing links to other documents.

Internet   The group of interconnected networks using TCP/IP protocols.

Internet telephony   A service that allows you to make long-distance telephone calls over the Internet.

InterNIC   Internet Network Information Center, a data and directory service funded by the government. Domain names are registered with InterNIC.

ISDN   Integrated services digital network; a service that offers digital data transfer speeds of either 64 bps or 128 bps over regular phone lines.

ISP   Internet service provider.

IT   Information technology.

Intranet   A private network inside an organization or company.

Java   A programming language using small Java programs, or applets, that can include functions such as animation.

LAN   Local-area network; a network linking computers and other devices within a small geographic area.

Mailing lists   Also known as discussion lists or listservs. An automated system that allows people to send E-mail to one address that automatically copies and re-mails the message to everyone who has subscribed to that particular list.

MMX   Multimedia extensions that allow PCs to deliver images quicker and in more TV-like fashion.

Modem   A device that allows computers to talk to other computers over phone lines or cable TV lines.

NAP   National access provider.

NAPs   Network access points, where the backbones connect and exchange information.

NSP   National service provider or national backbone operator.

Netiquette   Internet code of behavior.

Packet   A group of bytes traveling between hosts on the Internet. They may be of variable length and contain a variety of user information, but all contain information about where they came from and where they are going.

PC   Personal computer.

POP   Point of presence; a location where a network can be connected.

POTS   Plain old telephone service.

PPP   Point-to-point protocol; a fast, reliable method of connecting computers on the Internet.

Protocol   A set of rules used to define communications between computers.

Router   A networking device that uses software to examine packets of information to decide which path should be used to send information to its destination.

Search engine   A program that helps you find information on the Internet.

Server   A computer or software package providing a specific service to software running on other computers.

Shopping cart   Software that provides cataloging and ordering for an online store.

Site   A specific set of pages on the Internet.

Snail mail   Mail sent via the U.S. Postal Service as opposed to the nearly instant E-mail.

Spamming   E-mailing or posting inappropriate commercial messages.

Streaming   The processes of downloading and using a data file before the full file has been received.

Switch   A simple version of a router that uses hardware to direct traffic at high speeds.

Surf   To randomly search for information in the hopes of finding something new.

T-1   A digital phone line used for high-speed data transmission. It is not fast enough for full-screen, full-motion video.

T-3   The high-speed leased connection lines that may be used to link networks. They are fast enough for full-screen, full-motion video.

TCP/IP   Transfer control protocol/Internet protocol; standardized sets of computer guidelines that allow different computers to talk to each other.

URL   Uniform Resource Locator; a type of address that points to a specific site on the World Wide Web.

vBNS   Very high-speed Backbone Network System; the scientists' network.

VDSL   Very high speed digital subscriber line; transmits data in the 13 Mbps to 55 Mbps range. Not widely available.

VRML   Virtual reality modeling language; a language used to display three-dimensional information on the screen.

WAN   Wide-area network; a network of computers spread out over a great distance.

Wi-Fi   Wireless technology.

WWW   World Wide Web; a hypertext and hypermedia system. Also, the resources that can be accessed using Gopher, FTP, HTTP, and other tools.

About the Authors

•••

Marjorie Eberts has written more than seventy books. This is her twenty-fourth VGM Career Books title and her third book on careers associated with computers. She also has a syndicated newspaper column, "Dear Teacher," which appears in newspapers throughout the country. This is Rachel Kelsey's first career book. She has extensive experience with computers, especially in digital photography, word processing, and the construction of spreadsheets, and has written several software programs. Both Eberts and Kelsey are graduates of Stanford University.

Writing this book was a special pleasure for the authors, as it gave them the opportunity to spend hours online every day surfing the Net. They have visited every website mentioned in this book as well as many of the links to other sites. Almost everyone who was interviewed for this book was contacted by E-mail and responded to the authors' questions by E-mail. In addition, almost all of the research for this book was done on the Internet. The authors are truly cybersurfers.